Name ______________________________

EXERCISE 1-1

1. ______________
2. ______________
3. ______________
4. ______________
5. ______________
6. ______________
7. ______________
8. ______________
9. ______________
10. ______________
14. ______________
15. ______________

EXERCISE 1-2

1. ______________
2. ______________
3. ______________
4. ______________
5. ______________
6. ______________
7. ______________
8. ______________
9. ______________
10. ______________
11. ______________
12. ______________
13. ______________
14. ______________
15. ______________

EXERCISE 1-3

____

____

____

____

____

____

____

____

EXERCISE 1-4

1. ______________
2. ______________
3. ______________
4. ______________
5. ______________
6. ______________
7. ______________
8. ______________
9. ______________
10. ______________

EXERCISE 1-5

Coca-Cola owners' (stockholders') equity: ______________

PepsiCo owners' (stockholders') equity: ______________

EXERCISE 1-6

Toys "R" Us: ______________

Estée Lauder: ______________

EXERCISE 1-7

	Assets	=	Liabilities	+	Owner's Equity
a.	________	=	$25,000	+	$71,500
b.	$82,750	=	________	+	15,000
c.	37,000	=	17,500	+	________

EXERCISE 1-8

a. ____________________

b. ____________________

c. ____________________

d. ____________________

e. ____________________

EXERCISE 1-9

a. wages expense: ____________________

b. accounts payable: ____________________

c. cash: ____________________

d. land: ____________________

e. fees earned: ____________________

f. supplies: ____________________

EXERCISE 1-10

a. ____________________

b. ____________________

c. ____________________

d. ____________________

e. ____________________

EXERCISE 1-11

a. (1) Assets: ____________________

(2) Liabilities: ____________________

(3) Owners' equity: ____________________

b. (1) Assets: ____________________

(2) Liabilities: ____________________

(3) Owners' equity: ____________________

EXERCISE 1-12

1. revenues: ______________________________
2. expenses: ______________________________
3. issuance of capital stock: ______________________________
4. cash dividends: ______________________________

EXERCISE 1-13

1. ______________
2. ______________
3. ______________
4. ______________
5. ______________
6. ______________
7. ______________
8. ______________
9. ______________
10. ______________

EXERCISE 1-14

a. (1) ______________________________
(2) ______________________________
(3) ______________________________
(4) ______________________________
(5) ______________________________
(6) ______________________________
(7) ______________________________

b. ______________________________

c. ______________________________

d. ______________________________

e. ______________________________

EXERCISE 1-15

____
____
____
____
____
____
____
____
____

EXERCISE 1-16

Company M:

Company N:

Company O:

Company P:

EXERCISE 1-17

1. Supplies:

2. Wages Expense:

3. Cash:

4. Land:

5. Utilities Expense:

6. Fees Earned:

7. Supplies Expense:

8. Accounts Payable:

9. Capital Stock:

10. Wages Payable:

Name ____________________

EXERCISE 1-18

1. Supplies: ____________________
2. Wages Expense: ____________________
3. Cash: ____________________
4. Land: ____________________
5. Utilities Expense: ____________________
6. Fees Earned: ____________________
7. Supplies Expense: ____________________
8. Accounts Payable: ____________________
9. Capital Stock: ____________________
10. Wages Payable: ____________________

EXERCISE 1-19

EXERCISE 1-20

EXERCISE 1-21

	I	II	III	IV
Beginning of the year:				
Assets	$720,000	$125,000	$160,000	(d) $______
Liabilities	432,000	65,000	121,600	150,000
End of the year:				
Assets	894,000	175,000	144,000	310,000
Liabilities	390,000	55,000	128,000	170,000
During the year:				
Additional issue of capital stock	(a) ______	25,000	16,000	50,000
Dividends	48,000	8,000	(c) ______	75,000
Revenue	237,300	(b) ______	184,000	140,000
Expenses	129,600	32,000	196,000	160,000

Calculations:

EXERCISE 1-22

a.

DERBY INTERIORS

Balance Sheet

October 31, 2006

DERBY INTERIORS

Balance Sheet

November 30, 2006

EXERCISE 1-22, Concluded

b. ______________________________

c. ______________________________

EXERCISE 1-23

a. Operating expenses: ______________________________

b. Crude oil inventory: ______________________________

c. Income taxes payable: ______________________________

d. Sales: ______________________________

e. Investments: ______________________________

f. Marketable securities: ______________________________

g. Exploration expenses: ______________________________

h. Notes and loans payable: ______________________________

i. Cash equivalents: ______________________________

j. Long-term debt: ______________________________

k. Selling expenses: ______________________________

l. Notes receivable: ______________________________

m. Equipment: ______________________________

n. Accounts payable: ______________________________

o. Prepaid taxes: ______________________________

EXERCISE 1-24

1. Cash paid for land: ______________________________

2. Cash received from fees earned: ______________________________

3. Cash received as investment from stockholders: ______________________________

4. Cash paid for expenses: ______________________________

Name ____________________

EXERCISE 1-25

EXERCISE 1-26

a. 2003: ____________________

____

2002: ____________________

____

b. 2003: ____________________

____

2002: ____________________

c. ____________________

____

____

____

____

____

EXERCISE 1-27

a. 2003: ____________________

____

2002: ____________________

____

b. 2003: ____________________

____

2002: ____________________

c. ____________________

____

____

____

____

____

d.

____

____

____

____

____

____

Name ______________________________

PROBLEM 1-3 ___

1. *Omit "00" in the cents columns.*

2. *Omit "00" in the cents columns.*

PROBLEM 1-3 ___, Concluded

3. *Omit "00" in the cents columns.*

PROBLEM 1-6 ___

a. ______________________________

b. ______________________________

c. ______________________________

d. ______________________________

e. ______________________________

f. ______________________________

g. ______________________________

h. ______________________________

i. ______________________________

j. ______________________________

k. ______________________________

l. ______________________________

m. ______________________________

n. ______________________________

o. ______________________________

p. ______________________________

Page not used.

CONTINUING PROBLEM

1.

	Assets					=	Liabilities	+	Owners' Equity			
	Cash	+	Accounts Receivable	+	Supplies	=	Accounts Payable	+	Capital Stock	+	Retained Earnings	
Apr. 1												
2												
Bal.												
Apr. 2												
Bal.												
Apr. 4												
Bal.												
Apr. 6												
Bal.												
Apr. 8												
Bal.												
Apr. 12												
Bal.												
Apr. 13												
Bal.												
Apr. 16												
Bal.												
Apr. 22												
Bal.												
Apr. 25												
Bal.												
Apr. 29												
Bal.												
Apr. 30												
Bal.												
Apr. 30												
Bal.												
Apr. 30												
Bal.												
Apr. 30												
Bal.												
Apr. 30												
Bal.												
Apr. 30												
Bal.												
Apr. 30												
Bal.												

CONTINUING PROBLEM, Continued

2. *Omit "00" in the cents columns.*

3. *Omit "00" in the cents columns.*

CONTINUING PROBLEM, Concluded

4. *Omit "00" in the cents columns.*

Page not used.

EXERCISE 2-1

Accounts Payable: ____________________

Aircraft Fuel Expense: ____________________

Air Traffic Liability: ____________________

Cargo and Mail Revenue: ____________________

Commissions: ____________________

Flight Equipment: ____________________

Landing Fees: ____________________

Passenger Revenue: ____________________

Purchase Deposits for Flight Equipment: ____________________

Spare Parts and Supplies: ____________________

EXERCISE 2-2

Account	Account Number
Accounts Payable..................	________
Accounts Receivable.............	________
Capital Stock	________
Cash	________
Dividends..............................	________
Fees Earned..........................	________
Land......................................	________
Miscellaneous Expense	________
Supplies Expense..................	________
Wages Expense	________

EXERCISE 2-3

Balance Sheet Accounts

Acct #	Account Name

Income Statement Accounts

Acct #	Account Name

EXERCISE 2-4

a. and b.

	Account Debited		Account Credited	
Transaction	**Type**	**Effect**	**Type**	**Effect**
(1)	asset	+	capital stock	+
(2)				
(3)				
(4)				
(5)				
(6)				
(7)				
(8)				
(9)				

EXERCISE 2-5

JOURNAL PAGE

	DATE		DESCRIPTION	POST. REF.	DEBIT	CREDIT	
1							1
2							2
3							3
4							4
5							5
6							6
7							7
8							8
9							9
10							10
11							11
12							12
13							13
14							14
15							15
16							16
17							17
18							18
19							19
20							20
21							21
22							22

EXERCISE 2-5, Concluded

JOURNAL

PAGE

	DATE		DESCRIPTION	POST. REF.	DEBIT	CREDIT	
1							1
2							2
3							3
4							4
5							5
6							6
7							7

EXERCISE 2-6

EXERCISE 2-7

1. Accounts Payable: ________________________
2. Accounts Receivable: ________________________
3. Cash: ________________________
4. Fees Earned: ________________________
5. Dividends: ________________________
6. Insurance Expense: ________________________
7. Supplies Expense: ________________________

EXERCISE 2-8

a. Accounts Payable: ______

b. Accounts Receivable: ______

c. Cash: ______

d. Capital Stock: ______

e. Dividends: ______

f. Fees Earned: ______

g. Office Equipment: ______

h. Rent Expense: ______

i. Supplies: ______

j. Wages Expense: ______

EXERCISE 2-9

	Increase	Decrease	Normal Balance
Balance sheet accounts:			
Asset	Debit	(a) ______	Debit
Liability	(b) ______	(c) ______	(d) ______
Stockholders' Equity:			
Capital Stock	Credit	(e) ______	(f) ______
Retained Earnings	(g) ______	Debit	(h) ______
Dividends	(i) ______	Credit	(j) ______
Income statement accounts:			
Revenue	Credit	(k) ______	(l) ______
Expense	(m) ______	(n) ______	Debit

EXERCISE 2-10

a. ______

b. ______

______

______

______

EXERCISE 2-11

a. ______

______

______

b. ______

Name ______________________________

EXERCISE 2-12

a. ______________________________

b. ______________________________

c. ______________________________

EXERCISE 2-13

JOURNAL PAGE

	DATE	DESCRIPTION	POST. REF.	DEBIT	CREDIT	
1						1
2						2
3						3
4						4
5						5
6						6
7						7
8						8
9						9
10						10
11						11
12						12
13						13
14						14
15						15
16						16
17						17
18						18
19						19
20						20
21						21
22						22
23						23
24						24
25						25
26						26
27						27
28						28
29						29
30						30
31						31
32						32

EXERCISE 2-14

a.

JOURNAL

PAGE *29*

	DATE		DESCRIPTION	POST. REF.	DEBIT	CREDIT	
1							1
2							2
3							3

b.–d.

ACCOUNT ACCOUNT NO.

DATE		ITEM	POST. REF.	DEBIT	CREDIT	BALANCE DEBIT	BALANCE CREDIT

ACCOUNT ACCOUNT NO.

DATE		ITEM	POST. REF.	DEBIT	CREDIT	BALANCE DEBIT	BALANCE CREDIT

EXERCISE 2-15

a.

JOURNAL

PAGE

	DATE		DESCRIPTION	POST. REF.	DEBIT	CREDIT	
1							1
2							2
3							3
4							4
5							5
6							6
7							7
8							8
9							9
10							10
11							11
12							12
13							13
14							14

EXERCISE 2-15, Concluded

b.

Cash

Accounts Payable

Supplies

Fees Earned

Accounts Receivable

EXERCISE 2-16

EXERCISE 2-17

EXERCISE 2-18

EXERCISE 2-19

Error	(a) Out of Balance	(b) Difference	(c) Larger Total
1.	yes	$1,250	debit
2.			
3.			
4.			
5.			
6.			
7.			

EXERCISE 2-20

EXERCISE 2-21

a. and b.

JOURNAL PAGE

	DATE		DESCRIPTION	POST. REF.	DEBIT	CREDIT	
1							1
2							2
3							3
4							4
5							5

EXERCISE 2-22

a. and b.

JOURNAL PAGE

	DATE		DESCRIPTION	POST. REF.	DEBIT	CREDIT	
1							1
2							2
3							3
4							4
5							5
6							6
7							7
8							8
9							9

EXERCISE 2-23

a. 1. Net sales (revenues): ______________________

2. Total operating expenses: ______________________

b. ______________________

EXERCISE 2-24

a.

	2000	1999	INCREASE (DECREASE)	
			AMOUNT	PERCENT

b.

PROBLEM 2-1 ___

1. and 2.

Cash

Accounts Receivable

Supplies

Prepaid Insurance

Automobiles

PROBLEM 2-1 ___, Continued

Equipment

Notes Payable

Accounts Payable

Capital Stock

Professional Fees

Rent Expense

PROBLEM 2-1 ___, Continued

Salary Expense

Automobile Expense

Blueprint Expense

Miscellaneous Expense

PROBLEM 2-1 ___, Concluded

3.

Trial Balance

Name ____________________________________

PROBLEM 2-2 ___

1.

JOURNAL

PAGE

DATE	DESCRIPTION	POST. REF.	DEBIT	CREDIT

PROBLEM 2-2 ___, Continued

JOURNAL PAGE

	DATE	DESCRIPTION	POST. REF.	DEBIT	CREDIT	
1						1
2						2
3						3
4						4
5						5
6						6
7						7
8						8

2.

Cash

Supplies

Accounts Payable

Capital Stock

Name ______________________________

PROBLEM 2-2 ___, Continued

Dividends

Sales Commissions

Office Salaries Expense

Rent Expense

Automobile Expense

Supplies Expense

Miscellaneous Expense

PROBLEM 2-2 ___, Concluded

3.

Trial Balance

4. a. $ ______________________

b. $ ______________________

c. $ ______________________

PROBLEM 2-5 ___

JOURNAL

PAGE *19*

DATE		DESCRIPTION	POST. REF.	DEBIT	CREDIT
20— July	1	Rent Expense	54	1540.00	
		Cash	11		1540.00
	4	Supplies	12	149.00	
		Accounts Payable	22		149.00
	6	Advertising Expense	53	275.00	
		Cash	11		275.00
	8	Cash	11	1595.30	
		Service Revenue	41		1595.30
	9	Prepaid Insurance	13	144.00	
		Cash	11		144.00
	10	Land	16	12000.00	
		Cash	11		5500.00
		Notes Payable	21		6500.00
	13	Accounts Payable	22	847.20	
		Cash	11		847.20
	14	Miscellaneous Expense	58	162.10	
		Cash	11		162.10
	15	Wages Expense	51	1128.60	
		Cash	11		1128.60
	15	Cash	11	1785.50	
		Service Revenue	41		1785.50
	16	Dividends	33	750.00	
		Cash	11		750.00

PROBLEM 2-5 ___, Continued

JOURNAL

PAGE 20

DATE		DESCRIPTION	POST. REF.	DEBIT	CREDIT
20— July	17	Supplies	12	212 60	
		Accounts Payable	22		212 60
	20	Cash	11	1 662 20	
		Service Revenue	41		1 662 20
	22	Accounts Payable	22	74 20	
		Supplies	12		74 20
	25	Miscellaneous Expense	58	121 40	
		Cash	11		121 40
	25	Cash	11	1 681 30	
		Service Revenue	41		1 681 30
	30	Utilities Expense	52	436 60	
		Cash	11		436 60
	31	Wages Expense	51	1 390 00	
		Cash	11		1 390 00
	31	Dividends	33	600 00	
		Cash	11		600 00
	31	Cash	11	1 276 10	
		Service Revenue	41		1 276 10
6.					

Name ____________________________________

PROBLEM 2-5 ___, Continued

1. and 3.

ACCOUNT *Cash* ACCOUNT NO. *11*

DATE		ITEM	POST. REF.	DEBIT	CREDIT	BALANCE DEBIT	BALANCE CREDIT
20— July	1	Balance	√			13,810.50	
	1		19		1,540.00		
	6		19		275.00		
	8		19	1,595.30			
	9		19		144.00		
	10		19		5,500.00		
	13		19		847.20		
	14		19		162.10		
	15		19		1,128.60		
	15		19	1,875.50			
	16		19		750.00		
	20		20	1,662.20			
	25		20		121.40		
	25		20	1,681.30			
	30		20		436.60		
	31		20		1,390.00		
	31		20		600.00		
	31		20	1,276.10		9,006.00	

ACCOUNT *Supplies* ACCOUNT NO. *12*

DATE		ITEM	POST. REF.	DEBIT	CREDIT	BALANCE DEBIT	BALANCE CREDIT
20— July	1	Balance	√			710.50	
	4		19	149.00			
	17		20	212.60			
	22		20		74.20	997.90	

ACCOUNT *Prepaid Insurance* ACCOUNT NO. *13*

DATE		ITEM	POST. REF.	DEBIT	CREDIT	BALANCE DEBIT	BALANCE CREDIT
20— July	1	Balance	√			251.50	
	9		19	144.00		395.50	

PROBLEM 2-5 ___, Continued

ACCOUNT *Land* ACCOUNT NO. *16*

DATE		ITEM	POST. REF.	DEBIT	CREDIT	BALANCE DEBIT	BALANCE CREDIT
20— July	1	Balance	√	14,625 00		14,625 00	
	10		19	12,000 00		26,625 00	

ACCOUNT *Notes Payable* ACCOUNT NO. *21*

DATE		ITEM	POST. REF.	DEBIT	CREDIT	BALANCE DEBIT	BALANCE CREDIT
20— July	10		19		6,500 00		6,500 00

ACCOUNT *Accounts Payable* ACCOUNT NO. *22*

DATE		ITEM	POST. REF.	DEBIT	CREDIT	BALANCE DEBIT	BALANCE CREDIT
20— July	1	Balance	√				1,637 30
	4		19		149 00		
	13		19	847 20			
	17		20		212 60		
	22		20	74 20			1,077 50

ACCOUNT *Capital Stock* ACCOUNT NO. *31*

DATE		ITEM	POST. REF.	DEBIT	CREDIT	BALANCE DEBIT	BALANCE CREDIT
20— July	1	Balance	√				5,000 00

PROBLEM 2-5 ___, Continued

ACCOUNT *Retained Earnings* ACCOUNT NO. 32

DATE		ITEM	POST. REF.	DEBIT	CREDIT	BALANCE DEBIT	BALANCE CREDIT
20— July	1	Balance	√				20,260.20

ACCOUNT *Dividends* ACCOUNT NO. 33

DATE		ITEM	POST. REF.	DEBIT	CREDIT	BALANCE DEBIT	BALANCE CREDIT
20— July	16		19	750.00			
	31		20	600.00		1,500.00	

ACCOUNT *Service Revenue* ACCOUNT NO. 41

DATE		ITEM	POST. REF.	DEBIT	CREDIT	BALANCE DEBIT	BALANCE CREDIT
20— July	8		19		1,595.30		
	15		19		1,785.50		
	20		20		1,662.20		
	25		20		1,681.30		
	31		20		1,726.10		8,450.40

ACCOUNT *Wages Expense* ACCOUNT NO. 51

DATE		ITEM	POST. REF.	DEBIT	CREDIT	BALANCE DEBIT	BALANCE CREDIT
20— July	15		19	1,128.60			
	31		20	1,390.00		2,518.60	

PROBLEM 2-5 ___, Continued

ACCOUNT *Utilities Expense* ACCOUNT NO. *52*

DATE		ITEM	POST. REF.	DEBIT	CREDIT	BALANCE DEBIT	BALANCE CREDIT
20— July	30		20	4,366.00		4,366.00	

ACCOUNT *Advertising Expense* ACCOUNT NO. *53*

DATE		ITEM	POST. REF.	DEBIT	CREDIT	BALANCE DEBIT	BALANCE CREDIT
20— July	6		19	275.00		275.00	

ACCOUNT *Rent Expense* ACCOUNT NO. *54*

DATE		ITEM	POST. REF.	DEBIT	CREDIT	BALANCE DEBIT	BALANCE CREDIT
20— July	1		19	15,400.00		15,400.00	

ACCOUNT *Miscellaneous Expense* ACCOUNT NO. *58*

DATE		ITEM	POST. REF.	DEBIT	CREDIT	BALANCE DEBIT	BALANCE CREDIT
20— July	14		19	162.10			
	25		20	121.40		283.50	

PROBLEM 2-5 ___, Continued

CYPRESS TV REPAIR
Trial Balance
July 31, 20—

Cash	9,006 00	
Supplies	997 90	
Prepaid Insurance	395 50	
Land	26,265 00	
Notes Payable		6,500 00
Accounts Payable	1,077 50	
Capital Stock		7,500 00
Retained Earnings		20,260 20
Dividends	1,500 00	
Service Revenue		8,450 40
Wages Expense		2,518 60
Utilities Expense	4,366 00	
Rent Expense	15,400 00	
Miscellaneous Expense	283 50	
	59,291 40	45,229 20

PROBLEM 2-5 ___, Concluded

Verification Schedule

1. Totals of preliminary trial balance: Debit $ ______________

Credit $ ______________

2. Difference between preliminary trial balance totals: $ ______________

3. Errors in trial balance:

____

____

____

4. Errors in account balances:

____

____

____

5. Errors in posting:

____

____

____

7.

CYPRESS TV REPAIR

Trial Balance

July 31, 20—

Name ______________________________

PROBLEM 2-6 ___

1.

Trial Balance

Cash		
Accounts Receivable		
Supplies		
Prepaid Insurance		
Equipment		
Notes Payable		
Accounts Payable		
Capital Stock		
Retained Earnings		
Dividends		
Fees Earned		
Wages Expense		
Rent Expense		
Advertising Expense		
Gas, Electricity, and Water Expense		
Miscellaneous Expense		

PROBLEM 2-6 ___, Concluded

2.

Name ____________________________________

CONTINUING PROBLEM

2. and 3.

JOURNAL

PAGE *1*

DATE		DESCRIPTION	POST. REF.	DEBIT	CREDIT

CONTINUING PROBLEM, Continued

JOURNAL

PAGE 2

	DATE		DESCRIPTION	POST. REF.	DEBIT	CREDIT	
1							1
2							2
3							3
4							4
5							5
6							6
7							7
8							8
9							9
10							10
11							11
12							12
13							13
14							14
15							15
16							16
17							17
18							18
19							19
20							20
21							21
22							22
23							23
24							24
25							25
26							26
27							27
28							28
29							29
30							30
31							31
32							32
33							33
34							34
35							35
36							36

Name ____

CONTINUING PROBLEM, Continued

JOURNAL

PAGE 3

	DATE	DESCRIPTION	POST. REF.	DEBIT	CREDIT	
1						1
2						2
3						3
4						4
5						5
6						6
7						7
8						8
9						9
10						10
11						11
12						12
13						13
14						14
15						15
16						16
17						17
18						18
19						19
20						20
21						21
22						22
23						23
24						24
25						25
26						26
27						27
28						28
29						29
30						30
31						31
32						32
33						33
34						34
35						35
36						36

CONTINUING PROBLEM, Continued

1. and 3.

ACCOUNT *Cash* ACCOUNT NO. *11*

DATE	ITEM	POST. REF.	DEBIT	CREDIT	BALANCE DEBIT	BALANCE CREDIT

ACCOUNT *Accounts Receivable* ACCOUNT NO. *12*

DATE	ITEM	POST. REF.	DEBIT	CREDIT	BALANCE DEBIT	BALANCE CREDIT

CONTINUING PROBLEM, Continued

ACCOUNT *Supplies* ACCOUNT NO. *14*

DATE		ITEM	POST. REF.	DEBIT	CREDIT	BALANCE	
						DEBIT	CREDIT

ACCOUNT *Prepaid Insurance* ACCOUNT NO. *15*

DATE		ITEM	POST. REF.	DEBIT	CREDIT	BALANCE	
						DEBIT	CREDIT

ACCOUNT *Office Equipment* ACCOUNT NO. *17*

DATE		ITEM	POST. REF.	DEBIT	CREDIT	BALANCE	
						DEBIT	CREDIT

ACCOUNT *Accumulated Depreciation—Office Equipment* ACCOUNT NO. *18*

DATE		ITEM	POST. REF.	DEBIT	CREDIT	BALANCE	
						DEBIT	CREDIT

ACCOUNT *Accounts Payable* ACCOUNT NO. *21*

DATE		ITEM	POST. REF.	DEBIT	CREDIT	BALANCE	
						DEBIT	CREDIT

CONTINUING PROBLEM, Continued

ACCOUNT *Wages Payable* ACCOUNT NO. *22*

DATE		ITEM	POST. REF.	DEBIT	CREDIT	BALANCE DEBIT	BALANCE CREDIT

ACCOUNT *Unearned Revenue* ACCOUNT NO. *23*

DATE		ITEM	POST. REF.	DEBIT	CREDIT	BALANCE DEBIT	BALANCE CREDIT

ACCOUNT *Capital Stock* ACCOUNT NO. *31*

DATE		ITEM	POST. REF.	DEBIT	CREDIT	BALANCE DEBIT	BALANCE CREDIT

ACCOUNT *Retained Earnings* ACCOUNT NO. *32*

DATE		ITEM	POST. REF.	DEBIT	CREDIT	BALANCE DEBIT	BALANCE CREDIT

ACCOUNT *Dividends* ACCOUNT NO. *33*

DATE		ITEM	POST. REF.	DEBIT	CREDIT	BALANCE DEBIT	BALANCE CREDIT

CONTINUING PROBLEM, Continued

ACCOUNT *Income Summary* ACCOUNT NO. *34*

DATE		ITEM	POST. REF.	DEBIT	CREDIT	BALANCE DEBIT	BALANCE CREDIT

ACCOUNT *Fees Earned* ACCOUNT NO. *41*

DATE		ITEM	POST. REF.	DEBIT	CREDIT	BALANCE DEBIT	BALANCE CREDIT

ACCOUNT *Wages Expense* ACCOUNT NO. *50*

DATE		ITEM	POST. REF.	DEBIT	CREDIT	BALANCE DEBIT	BALANCE CREDIT

ACCOUNT *Office Rent Expense* ACCOUNT NO. *51*

DATE		ITEM	POST. REF.	DEBIT	CREDIT	BALANCE DEBIT	BALANCE CREDIT

CONTINUING PROBLEM, Continued

ACCOUNT *Equipment Rent Expense* ACCOUNT NO. *52*

DATE		ITEM	POST. REF.	DEBIT	CREDIT	BALANCE	
						DEBIT	CREDIT

ACCOUNT *Utilities Expense* ACCOUNT NO. *53*

DATE		ITEM	POST. REF.	DEBIT	CREDIT	BALANCE	
						DEBIT	CREDIT

ACCOUNT *Music Expense* ACCOUNT NO. *54*

DATE		ITEM	POST. REF.	DEBIT	CREDIT	BALANCE	
						DEBIT	CREDIT

ACCOUNT *Advertising Expense* ACCOUNT NO. *55*

DATE		ITEM	POST. REF.	DEBIT	CREDIT	BALANCE	
						DEBIT	CREDIT

CONTINUING PROBLEM, Continued

ACCOUNT *Supplies Expense* ACCOUNT NO. *56*

DATE		ITEM	POST. REF.	DEBIT	CREDIT	BALANCE DEBIT	BALANCE CREDIT

ACCOUNT *Insurance Expense* ACCOUNT NO. *57*

DATE		ITEM	POST. REF.	DEBIT	CREDIT	BALANCE DEBIT	BALANCE CREDIT

ACCOUNT *Depreciation Expense* ACCOUNT NO. *58*

DATE		ITEM	POST. REF.	DEBIT	CREDIT	BALANCE DEBIT	BALANCE CREDIT

ACCOUNT *Miscellaneous Expense* ACCOUNT NO. *59*

DATE		ITEM	POST. REF.	DEBIT	CREDIT	BALANCE DEBIT	BALANCE CREDIT

CONTINUING PROBLEM, Concluded

4.

Trial Balance

EXERCISE 3-1

1. Salary owed but not yet paid: ____________________
2. Supplies on hand: ____________________
3. Fees received but not yet earned: ____________________
4. Fees earned but not yet received: ____________________
5. Taxes owed but payable in the following period: ____________________
6. Utilities owed but not yet paid: ____________________
7. A two-year premium paid on a fire insurance policy: ____________________
8. Subscriptions received in advance by a magazine publisher: ____________________

EXERCISE 3-2

Account	Answer
Dividends	Does not normally require adjustment.
Accounts Receivable	Normally requires adjustment (AR).
Accumulated Depreciation	
Cash	
Interest Payable	
Interest Receivable	
Land	
Office Equipment	
Prepaid Rent	
Supplies Expense	
Unearned Fees	
Wages Expense	

EXERCISE 3-3

JOURNAL PAGE

	DATE	DESCRIPTION	POST. REF.	DEBIT	CREDIT	
1						1
2						2
3						3

EXERCISE 3-4

____

____

EXERCISE 3-5

a. ______________________________

____

____

b. ______________________________

____

____

EXERCISE 3-6

a. and b.

JOURNAL PAGE

	DATE		DESCRIPTION	POST. REF.	DEBIT	CREDIT	
1							1
2							2
3							3
4							4
5							5
6							6

EXERCISE 3-7

a. and b.

JOURNAL PAGE

	DATE		DESCRIPTION	POST. REF.	DEBIT	CREDIT	
1							1
2							2
3							3
4							4
5							5
6							6

EXERCISE 3-8

JOURNAL PAGE

	DATE		DESCRIPTION	POST. REF.	DEBIT	CREDIT	
1							1
2							2
3							3

EXERCISE 3-9

a. ______________________________

____

____

b. ______________________________

____

____

EXERCISE 3-10

a. and b.

JOURNAL PAGE

	DATE		DESCRIPTION	POST. REF.	DEBIT	CREDIT	
1							1
2							2
3							3
4							4
5							5
6							6
7							7

EXERCISE 3-11

____

____

EXERCISE 3-12

a. ______________________________

____

b. ______________________________

____

EXERCISE 3-13

a. ______________________________

____

b. ______________________________

____

____

 Courtney Roons 6-15-05

EXERCISE 3-14

a.

JOURNAL PAGE

	DATE		DESCRIPTION	POST. REF.	DEBIT	CREDIT	
1	Dec.	31	License Tax Expense		945.00		1
2			Prepaid Licensed tax			945.00	2
3		31	Property tax expense		8750.00		3
4			Property tax Payable			8750.00	4
5							5
6							6
7							7
8							8

b. ______

EXERCISE 3-15

______

EXERCISE 3-16

a. ______

b. ______

EXERCISE 3-17

	Error (a) Over-stated	Error (a) Under-stated	Error (b) Over-stated	Error (b) Under-stated
1. Revenue for the year would be	$	$	$	$
2. Expenses for the year would be	$	$	$	$
3. Net income for the year would be	$	$	$	$
4. Assets at December 31 would be	$	$	$	$
5. Liabilities at December 31 would be	$	$	$	$
6. Stockholders' equity at December 31 would be	$	$	$	$

Name Courtney Koons 6-15-05

EXERCISE 3-18

EXERCISE 3-19

a.

JOURNAL PAGE

	DATE		DESCRIPTION	POST. REF.	DEBIT	CREDIT	
1			Accounts Receivable		1150000		1
2			Revenue Account			1150000	2
3							3
4							4

b.

EXERCISE 3-20

a. and b.

JOURNAL PAGE

	DATE		DESCRIPTION	POST. REF.	DEBIT	CREDIT	
1							1
2							2
3							3
4							4
5							5
6							6

EXERCISE 3-21

a.

b.

EXERCISE 3-22

JOURNAL

PAGE

	DATE		DESCRIPTION	POST. REF.	DEBIT	CREDIT	
1							1
2							2
3							3

EXERCISE 3-23

a.

b.

EXERCISE 3-24

a.

b.

EXERCISE 3-25

a.

JOURNAL

PAGE

	DATE		DESCRIPTION	POST. REF.	DEBIT	CREDIT	
1							1
2							2
3							3

b. (1)

(2)

EXERCISE 3-26

1.–5.

JOURNAL PAGE

	DATE		DESCRIPTION	POST. REF.	DEBIT	CREDIT	
1							1
2							2
3							3
4							4
5							5
6							6
7							7
8							8
9							9
10							10
11							11
12							12
13							13
14							14

EXERCISE 3-27

EXERCISE 3-28

a. 1. ______________________________

____

2. 2003: ______________________________

2002: ______________________________

b. ______________________________

____

____

____

____

EXERCISE 3-29

a. and b.

____

____

____

	DELL		GATEWAY	
	AMOUNT	PERCENT	AMOUNT	PERCENT

c. ______________________________

____

____

____

____

____

____

____

____

____

____

____

Name Courtney Koons

PROBLEM 3-1 A

1.

JOURNAL

PAGE

	DATE		DESCRIPTION	POST. REF.	DEBIT	CREDIT
accrued rev.	Aug.	31	Accounts Receivable		7,100.00	
		a)	Fees Earned			7,100.00
deferral exp		31	Supplies Expense		1,860.00	
		b)	Supplies			1,860.00
accruals expense		31	Wages Expens		1,380.00	
		c)	Wages Payable			1,380.00
deferred rev		31	Unearned Rent		1,650.00	
		d)	Rent Revenue			1,650.00
deprec.		31	Depreciation Expense		1,120.00	
		e)	Accumulated Depreciation			1,120.00

PROBLEM 3-1, Concluded

2.

PROBLEM 3-2 ___

JOURNAL

PAGE

DATE		DESCRIPTION	POST. REF.	DEBIT	CREDIT

Page not used.

PROBLEM 3-3 ___

JOURNAL

PAGE

	DATE	DESCRIPTION	POST. REF.	DEBIT	CREDIT	
1						1
2						2
3						3
4						4
5						5
6						6
7						7
8						8
9						9
10						10
11						11
12						12
13						13
14						14
15						15
16						16
17						17
18						18
19						19
20						20
21						21
22						22
23						23
24						24
25						25
26						26
27						27
28						28
29						29
30						30
31						31
32						32
33						33
34						34
35						35
36						36

Page not used.

Name Courtney Koons

PROBLEM 3-4 ___

JOURNAL

PAGE

DATE		DESCRIPTION	POST. REF.	DEBIT	CREDIT

Page not used.

Name Courtney Koons

PROBLEM 3-5 ___

1.

JOURNAL

PAGE

DATE		DESCRIPTION	POST. REF.	DEBIT	CREDIT

PROBLEM 3-5 ___, Concluded

2.

Adjusted Trial Balance

PROBLEM 3-6 ___

1.

JOURNAL

PAGE

DATE		DESCRIPTION	POST. REF.	DEBIT	CREDIT

PROBLEM 3-6 ___, Concluded

2.

	Net Income	Total Assets	Total Liabilities	Total Stockholders' Equity
Reported amounts	$	$	$	$
Corrections:				
Adjustment (a)				
Adjustment (b)				
Adjustment (c)				
Adjustment (d)				
Corrected amounts	$	$	$	$

CONTINUING PROBLEM

1.

JOURNAL

PAGE

DATE		DESCRIPTION	POST. REF.	DEBIT	CREDIT

CONTINUING PROBLEM, Concluded

2. Note: Use the general ledger accounts provided in Chapter 2, pages 78–83.

3.

Adjusted Trial Balance

Name ______________________________

EXERCISE 4-1

1. ______________________
2. ______________________
3. ______________________
4. ______________________
5. ______________________
6. ______________________
7. ______________________

EXERCISE 4-2

1. Accounts Payable: ______________________
2. Accounts Receivable: ______________________
3. Dividends: ______________________
4. Fees Earned: ______________________
5. Retained Earnings: ______________________
6. Supplies: ______________________
7. Unearned Fees: ______________________
8. Utilities Expense: ______________________
9. Wages Expense: ______________________
10. Wages Payable: ______________________

EXERCISE 4-3

1. Accounts Receivable: ______________________
2. Fees Earned: ______________________
3. Insurance Expense: ______________________
4. Land: ______________________
5. Prepaid Advertising: ______________________
6. Prepaid Insurance: ______________________
7. Rent Revenue: ______________________
8. Salary Expense: ______________________
9. Salary Payable: ______________________
10. Supplies: ______________________
11. Supplies Expense: ______________________
12. Unearned Rent: ______________________

EXERCISE 4-4

1. ______________________
2. ______________________
3. ______________________
4. ______________________
5. ______________________
6. ______________________
7. ______________________
8. ______________________
9. ______________________
10. ______________________

EXERCISE 4-5

Ithaca Services Co.
Work Sheet
For the Year Ended January 31, 2006

Account Title	Trial Balance Dr.	Trial Balance Cr.	Adjustments Dr.	Adjustments Cr.	Adjusted Trial Balance Dr.	Adjusted Trial Balance Cr.
Cash	8					
Accounts Receivable	50					
Supplies	8					
Prepaid Insurance	12					
Land	50					
Equipment	32					
Accumulated Depr.—Equip.		2				
Accounts Payable		26				
Wages Payable		0				
Capital Stock		20				
Retained Earnings		92				
Dividends	8					
Fees Earned		60				
Wages Expense	16					
Rent Expense	8					
Insurance Expense	0					
Utilities Expense	6					
Depreciation Expense	0					
Supplies Expense	0					
Miscellaneous Expense	2					
Totals	200	200				

EXERCISE 4-6

Ithaca Services Co.
Work Sheet
For the Year Ended January 31, 2006

Account Title	Adjusted Trial Balance Dr.	Adjusted Trial Balance Cr.	Income Statement Dr.	Income Statement Cr.	Balance Sheet Dr.	Balance Sheet Cr.
Cash	8					
Accounts Receivable	57					
Supplies	3					
Prepaid Insurance	6					
Land	50					
Equipment	32					
Accumulated Depr.—Equip.		7				
Accounts Payable		26				
Wages Payable		1				
Capital Stock		20				
Retained Earnings		92				
Dividends	8					
Fees Earned		67				
Wages Expense	17					
Rent Expense	8					
Insurance Expense	6					
Utilities Expense	6					
Depreciation Expense	5					
Supplies Expense	5					
Miscellaneous Expense	2					
Totals	213	213				
Net income (loss)						

EXERCISE 4-7

Income Statement

Retained Earnings Statement

EXERCISE 4-7, Concluded

Balance Sheet

EXERCISE 4-8

JOURNAL

PAGE

	DATE	DESCRIPTION	POST. REF.	DEBIT	CREDIT	
1						1
2						2
3						3
4						4
5						5
6						6
7						7
8						8
9						9
10						10
11						11
12						12
13						13
14						14

EXERCISE 4-9

JOURNAL

PAGE

	DATE	DESCRIPTION	POST. REF.	DEBIT	CREDIT	
1						1
2						2
3						3
4						4
5						5
6						6
7						7
8						8
9						9
10						10
11						11
12						12
13						13
14						14
15						15
16						16
17						17

Name ______________________________

EXERCISE 4-10

EXERCISE 4-11

EXERCISE 4-12

a.

b.

EXERCISE 4-13

EXERCISE 4-14

EXERCISE 4-15

1. Cash: ______________________
2. Equipment: ______________________
3. Accounts receivable: ______________________
4. Building: ______________________
5. Prepaid insurance: ______________________
6. Supplies: ______________________

EXERCISE 4-16

EXERCISE 4-17

EXERCISE 4-18

EXERCISE 4-18, Concluded

Name ______________________________

EXERCISE 4-19

JOURNAL

PAGE

DATE	DESCRIPTION	POST. REF.	DEBIT	CREDIT

EXERCISE 4-20

a. Accounts Payable: ______________________________

b. Accumulated Depreciation—Equipment: ______________________________

c. Capital Stock: ______________________________

d. Depreciation Expense—Equipment: ______________________________

e. Dividends: ______________________________

f. Equipment: ______________________________

g. Fees Earned: ______________________________

h. Land: ______________________________

i. Salaries Expense: ______________________________

j. Salaries Payable: ______________________________

k. Supplies: ______________________________

l. Supplies Expense: ______________________________

EXERCISE 4-21

EXERCISE 4-22

a.

JOURNAL PAGE

	DATE		DESCRIPTION	POST. REF.	DEBIT	CREDIT	
1							1
2							2
3							3
4							4
5							5

b.

EXERCISE 4-23

JOURNAL PAGE

	DATE		DESCRIPTION	POST. REF.	DEBIT	CREDIT	
1							1
2							2
3							3
4							4
5							5
6							6
7							7
8							8
9							9
10							10
11							11
12							12
13							13
14							14

EXERCISE 4-24

a. Accounts Receivable: ______________________________

b. Accumulated Depreciation: ______________________________

c. Capital Stock: ______________________________

d. Cash: ______________________________

e. Depreciation Expense: ______________________________

f.Dividends: ______________________________

g. Equipment: ______________________________

h. Fees Earned: ______________________________

i. Retained Earnings

j. Supplies: ______________________________

k. Wages Expense: ______________________________

l. Wages Payable: ______________________________

EXERCISE 4-25

EXERCISE 4-26

a. 2003 working capital: ______________________________

2002 working capital: ______________________________

2003 current ratio: ______________________________

2002 current ratio: ______________________________

b.

EXERCISE 4-27

a. 2002 working capital: ______________________________

2001 working capital: ______________________________

2002 current ratio: ______________________________

2001 current ratio: ______________________________

b.

APPENDIX EXERCISE 4-28

a.- b. **JOURNAL** PAGE

	DATE		DESCRIPTION	POST. REF.	DEBIT	CREDIT	
1							1
2							2
3							3
4							4
5							5
6							6
7							7
8							8
9							9
10							10
11							11

APPENDIX EXERCISE 4-29

a. (1) ______________________

(2) ______________________

(3) ______________________

(4) ______________________

(5) ______________________

b.(1)-(5) **JOURNAL** PAGE

	DATE		DESCRIPTION	POST. REF.	DEBIT	CREDIT	
1							1
2							2
3							3
4							4
5							5
6							6
7							7
8							8
9							9
10							10
11							11
12							12
13							13
14							14

Page not used.

Page not used.

PROBLEM 4-1 ___

1.

	ACCOUNT TITLE	TRIAL BALANCE		ADJUSTMENTS		
		DEBIT	CREDIT	DEBIT	CREDIT	
1						1
2						2
3						3
4						4
5						5
6						6
7						7
8						8
9						9
10						10
11						11
12						12
13						13
14						14
15						15
16						16
17						17
18						18
19						19
20						20
21						21
22						22
23						23
24						24
25						25
26						26
27						27
28						28
29						29
30						30
31						31
32						32
33						33
34						34

Name ______________________________

PROBLEM 4-1 ___, Continued

	ADJUSTED TRIAL BALANCE		INCOME STATEMENT		BALANCE SHEET		
	DEBIT	CREDIT	DEBIT	CREDIT	DEBIT	CREDIT	
1							1
2							2
3							3
4							4
5							5
6							6
7							7
8							8
9							9
10							10
11							11
12							12
13							13
14							14
15							15
16							16
17							17
18							18
19							19
20							20
21							21
22							22
23							23
24							24
25							25
26							26
27							27
28							28
29							29
30							30
31							31
32							32
33							33
34							34

Page not used.

PROBLEM 4-1 ___, Continued

2. *Omit "00" in the cents columns.*

Income Statement

Retained Earnings Statement

PROBLEM 4-1 ___, Continued

Balance Sheet

PROBLEM 4-1 ___, Continued

3.

JOURNAL PAGE

	DATE		DESCRIPTION	POST. REF.	DEBIT	CREDIT	
1			*Adjusting Entries*				1
2							2
3							3
4							4
5							5
6							6
7							7
8							8
9							9
10							10
11							11
12							12
13							13
14							14
15							15
16							16
17							17
18							18
19							19
20							20
21							21
22							22
23							23
24							24
25							25
26							26
27							27
28							28
29							29
30							30
31							31
32							32
33							33
34							34
35							35
36							36

PROBLEM 4-1 ___, Concluded

4.

JOURNAL

PAGE

	DATE		DESCRIPTION	POST. REF.	DEBIT	CREDIT	
1			*Closing Entries*				1
2							2
3							3
4							4
5							5
6							6
7							7
8							8
9							9
10							10
11							11
12							12
13							13
14							14
15							15
16							16
17							17
18							18
19							19
20							20
21							21
22							22
23							23
24							24
25							25
26							26
27							27
28							28
29							29
30							30
31							31
32							32
33							33
34							34
35							35
36							36

Name ______________________________

PROBLEM 4-2 ___

1.

JOURNAL PAGE

DATE		DESCRIPTION	POST. REF.	DEBIT	CREDIT
		Closing Entries			

PROBLEM 4-2 ___, Concluded

2. *Omit "00" in the cents columns.*

3.

Page not used.

PROBLEM 4-3 ___

1.

ACCOUNT TITLE	TRIAL BALANCE DEBIT	TRIAL BALANCE CREDIT	ADJUSTMENTS DEBIT	ADJUSTMENTS CREDIT
Cash	*4509 00*			
Accounts Receivable	*2550 00*			
Supplies	*1647 00*			
Prepaid Insurance	*1800 00*			
Land	*20000 00*			
Building	*55500 00*			
Accum. Depr.—Building		*23400 00*		
Equipment	*30000 00*			
Accum. Depr.—Equipment		*10200 00*		
Accounts Payable		*5141 00*		
Unearned Rent		*2200 00*		
Capital Stock		*7500 00*		
Retained Earnings		*50325 00*		
Dividends	*2000 00*			
Service Revenue		*41984 00*		
Wages Expense	*14799 00*			
Rent Expense	*3910 00*			
Utilities Expense	*1728 00*			
Miscellaneous Expense	*2307 00*			
	140750 00	*140750 00*		

Name ______________________________

PROBLEM 4-3 ___, Continued

ADJUSTED TRIAL BALANCE		INCOME STATEMENT		BALANCE SHEET	
DEBIT	CREDIT	DEBIT	CREDIT	DEBIT	CREDIT

Page not used.

Name ______________________________________

PROBLEM 4-3 ___, Continued

2.

Income Statement

Retained Earnings Statement

PROBLEM 4-3 ___, Continued

Balance Sheet

PROBLEM 4-3 ___, Continued

3.

JOURNAL

PAGE *26*

DATE		DESCRIPTION	POST. REF.	DEBIT	CREDIT
		Adjusting Entries			

PROBLEM 4-3 ___, Continued

4.

JOURNAL

PAGE *27*

DATE		DESCRIPTION	POST. REF.	DEBIT	CREDIT
		Closing Entries			

PROBLEM 4-3 ___, Continued

3. and 4.

ACCOUNT *Cash* ACCOUNT NO. *11*

DATE		ITEM	POST. REF.	DEBIT	CREDIT	BALANCE DEBIT	BALANCE CREDIT
2006 Mar.	1	Balance	√			2 259 00	
	3		23		910 00	1 349 00	
	4		23	5 000 00		6 349 00	
	5		23		86 00	6 263 00	
	7		23	800 00		7 063 00	
	8		23	400 00		7 463 00	
	8		23		2 584 00	4 879 00	
	8		23	1 695 00		6 574 00	
	10		24		510 00	6 064 00	
	12		24		2 319 00	3 745 00	
	15		24	2 718 00		6 463 00	
	16		24		1 000 00	5 463 00	
	19		24		2 135 00	3 328 00	
	22		24		370 00	2 958 00	
	22		24	3 992 00		6 950 00	
	24		25		527 00	6 423 00	
	26		25		2 480 00	3 943 00	
	30		25		156 00	3 787 00	
	30		25		26 00	3 761 00	
	31		25		1 000 00	2 761 00	
	31		25	2 029 00		4 790 00	
	31		25		281 00	4 509 00	

ACCOUNT *Accounts Receivable* ACCOUNT NO. *12*

DATE		ITEM	POST. REF.	DEBIT	CREDIT	BALANCE DEBIT	BALANCE CREDIT
2006 Mar.	1	Balance	√			2 200 00	
	7		23		800 00	1 400 00	
	8		23		400 00	1 000 00	
	22		24	1 550 00		2 550 00	

PROBLEM 4-3 ___, Continued

ACCOUNT *Supplies* ACCOUNT NO. *13*

DATE		ITEM	POST. REF.	DEBIT	CREDIT	BALANCE DEBIT	BALANCE CREDIT
2006 Mar.	1	Balance	√			610 00	
	10		24	510 00		1 120 00	
	27		25	527 00		1 647 00	

ACCOUNT *Prepaid Insurance* ACCOUNT NO. *14*

DATE		ITEM	POST. REF.	DEBIT	CREDIT	BALANCE DEBIT	BALANCE CREDIT
2006 Mar.	1	Balance	√			420 00	
	22		24	1 380 00		1 800 00	

ACCOUNT *Land* ACCOUNT NO. *15*

DATE		ITEM	POST. REF.	DEBIT	CREDIT	BALANCE DEBIT	BALANCE CREDIT
2006 Mar.	1	Balance	√			20 000 00	

ACCOUNT *Building* ACCOUNT NO. *16*

DATE		ITEM	POST. REF.	DEBIT	CREDIT	BALANCE DEBIT	BALANCE CREDIT
2006 Mar.	1	Balance	√			55 500 00	

PROBLEM 4-3 ___, Continued

ACCOUNT *Accumulated Depreciation—Building* ACCOUNT NO. *17*

DATE		ITEM	POST. REF.	DEBIT	CREDIT	BALANCE DEBIT	BALANCE CREDIT
2006 Mar.	1	Balance	√				23,400.00

ACCOUNT *Equipment* ACCOUNT NO. *18*

DATE		ITEM	POST. REF.	DEBIT	CREDIT	BALANCE DEBIT	BALANCE CREDIT
2006 Mar.	1	Balance	√			29,250.00	
	3		23	750.00		30,000.00	

ACCOUNT *Accumulated Depreciation—Equipment* ACCOUNT NO. *19*

DATE		ITEM	POST. REF.	DEBIT	CREDIT	BALANCE DEBIT	BALANCE CREDIT
2006 Mar.	1	Balance	√				10,200.00

ACCOUNT *Accounts Payable* ACCOUNT NO. *21*

DATE		ITEM	POST. REF.	DEBIT	CREDIT	BALANCE DEBIT	BALANCE CREDIT
2006 Mar.	1	Balance	√				8,625.00
	3		23		750.00		9,375.00
	8		23	2,584.00			6,791.00
	19		24	2,135.00			4,656.00
	31		25		485.00		5,141.00

PROBLEM 4-3 ___, Continued

ACCOUNT *Wages Payable* ACCOUNT NO. 22

DATE		ITEM	POST. REF.	DEBIT	CREDIT	BALANCE DEBIT	BALANCE CREDIT

ACCOUNT *Unearned Rent* ACCOUNT NO. 23

DATE		ITEM	POST. REF.	DEBIT	CREDIT	BALANCE DEBIT	BALANCE CREDIT
2006 Mar.	1	Balance	√				2,200.00

ACCOUNT *Capital Stock* ACCOUNT NO. 31

DATE		ITEM	POST. REF.	DEBIT	CREDIT	BALANCE DEBIT	BALANCE CREDIT
2006 Mar.	1	Balance	√				7,500.00

ACCOUNT *Retained Earnings* ACCOUNT NO. 32

DATE		ITEM	POST. REF.	DEBIT	CREDIT	BALANCE DEBIT	BALANCE CREDIT
2006 Mar.	1	Balance	√				50,325.00

PROBLEM 4-3 ___, Continued

ACCOUNT *Dividends* ACCOUNT NO. *33*

DATE		ITEM	POST. REF.	DEBIT	CREDIT	BALANCE DEBIT	BALANCE CREDIT
2006 Mar.	16		24	1,000 00		1,000 00	
	31		25	1,000 00		2,000 00	

ACCOUNT *Income Summary* ACCOUNT NO. *34*

DATE		ITEM	POST. REF.	DEBIT	CREDIT	BALANCE DEBIT	BALANCE CREDIT

ACCOUNT *Service Revenue* ACCOUNT NO. *41*

DATE		ITEM	POST. REF.	DEBIT	CREDIT	BALANCE DEBIT	BALANCE CREDIT
2006 Mar.	8		23		9,695 00		9,695 00
	15		24		7,718 00		17,413 00
	22		24		8,992 00		26,405 00
	22		24		7,550 00		33,955 00
	31		25		8,029 00		41,984 00

PROBLEM 4-3 ___, Continued

ACCOUNT *Rent Revenue* ACCOUNT NO. *42*

DATE		ITEM	POST. REF.	DEBIT	CREDIT	BALANCE DEBIT	BALANCE CREDIT

ACCOUNT *Wages Expense* ACCOUNT NO. *51*

DATE		ITEM	POST. REF.	DEBIT	CREDIT	BALANCE DEBIT	BALANCE CREDIT
2006 Mar.	*12*		*24*	*7,319.00*		*7,319.00*	
	26		*25*	*7,480.00*		*14,799.00*	

ACCOUNT *Supplies Expense* ACCOUNT NO. *52*

DATE		ITEM	POST. REF.	DEBIT	CREDIT	BALANCE DEBIT	BALANCE CREDIT

ACCOUNT *Rent Expense* ACCOUNT NO. *53*

DATE		ITEM	POST. REF.	DEBIT	CREDIT	BALANCE DEBIT	BALANCE CREDIT
2006 Mar.	*3*		*23*	*3,910.00*		*3,910.00*	

PROBLEM 4-3 ___, Continued

ACCOUNT *Depreciation Expense—Building* ACCOUNT NO. *54*

DATE		ITEM	POST. REF.	DEBIT	CREDIT	BALANCE DEBIT	BALANCE CREDIT

ACCOUNT *Utilities Expense* ACCOUNT NO. *55*

DATE		ITEM	POST. REF.	DEBIT	CREDIT	BALANCE DEBIT	BALANCE CREDIT
2006 Mar.	*5*		*24*	*586 00*		*586 00*	
	30		*25*	*456 00*		*1 042 00*	
	31		*25*	*686 00*		*1 728 00*	

ACCOUNT *Depreciation Expense—Equipment* ACCOUNT NO. *56*

DATE		ITEM	POST. REF.	DEBIT	CREDIT	BALANCE DEBIT	BALANCE CREDIT

ACCOUNT *Insurance Expense* ACCOUNT NO. *57*

DATE		ITEM	POST. REF.	DEBIT	CREDIT	BALANCE DEBIT	BALANCE CREDIT

PROBLEM 4-3 ___, Concluded

ACCOUNT *Miscellaneous Expense* ACCOUNT NO. *59*

DATE		ITEM	POST. REF.	DEBIT	CREDIT	BALANCE DEBIT	BALANCE CREDIT
2006 Mar.	30		25	1,026.00		1,026.00	
	31		25	1,281.00		2,307.00	

5.

Page not used.

PROBLEM 4-4 ___

1.

ACCOUNT TITLE	TRIAL BALANCE		ADJUSTMENTS	
	DEBIT	CREDIT	DEBIT	CREDIT

Name ____

PROBLEM 4-4 ___, Continued

____

____

____

	ADJUSTED TRIAL BALANCE		INCOME STATEMENT		BALANCE SHEET		
	DEBIT	CREDIT	DEBIT	CREDIT	DEBIT	CREDIT	
1							1
2							2
3							3
4							4
5							5
6							6
7							7
8							8
9							9
10							10
11							11
12							12
13							13
14							14
15							15
16							16
17							17
18							18
19							19
20							20
21							21
22							22
23							23
24							24
25							25
26							26
27							27
28							28
29							29
30							30
31							31
32							32
33							33
34							34

Page not used.

PROBLEM 4-4 ___, Continued

2.

JOURNAL

PAGE

DATE		DESCRIPTION	POST. REF.	DEBIT	CREDIT

PROBLEM 4-4 ___, Continued

3. *Omit "00" in the cents columns.*

Adjusted Trial Balance

PROBLEM 4-4 ___, Continued

4. *Omit "00" in the cents columns.*

5. *Omit "00" in the cents columns.*

PROBLEM 4-4 ___, Concluded

6.

7. ____________________%

Page not used.

PROBLEM 4-5 ___

2.

ACCOUNT TITLE	TRIAL BALANCE		ADJUSTMENTS	
	DEBIT	CREDIT	DEBIT	CREDIT

PROBLEM 4-5 ___, Continued

ADJUSTED TRIAL BALANCE		INCOME STATEMENT		BALANCE SHEET	
DEBIT	CREDIT	DEBIT	CREDIT	DEBIT	CREDIT

Page not used.

PROBLEM 4-5 ___, Continued

1., 3., and 6.

ACCOUNT *Cash* ACCOUNT NO. *11*

DATE		ITEM	POST. REF.	DEBIT	CREDIT	BALANCE	
						DEBIT	CREDIT

ACCOUNT *Supplies* ACCOUNT NO. *13*

DATE		ITEM	POST. REF.	DEBIT	CREDIT	BALANCE	
						DEBIT	CREDIT

ACCOUNT *Prepaid Insurance* ACCOUNT NO. *14*

DATE		ITEM	POST. REF.	DEBIT	CREDIT	BALANCE	
						DEBIT	CREDIT

ACCOUNT *Equipment* ACCOUNT NO. *16*

DATE		ITEM	POST. REF.	DEBIT	CREDIT	BALANCE	
						DEBIT	CREDIT

ACCOUNT *Accumulated Depreciation—Equipment* ACCOUNT NO. *17*

DATE		ITEM	POST. REF.	DEBIT	CREDIT	BALANCE	
						DEBIT	CREDIT

PROBLEM 4-5 ___, Continued

ACCOUNT *Trucks* ACCOUNT NO. *18*

DATE		ITEM	POST. REF.	DEBIT	CREDIT	BALANCE	
						DEBIT	CREDIT

ACCOUNT *Accumulated Depreciation—Trucks* ACCOUNT NO. *19*

DATE		ITEM	POST. REF.	DEBIT	CREDIT	BALANCE	
						DEBIT	CREDIT

ACCOUNT *Accounts Payable* ACCOUNT NO. *21*

DATE		ITEM	POST. REF.	DEBIT	CREDIT	BALANCE	
						DEBIT	CREDIT

ACCOUNT *Wages Payable* ACCOUNT NO. *22*

DATE		ITEM	POST. REF.	DEBIT	CREDIT	BALANCE	
						DEBIT	CREDIT

ACCOUNT *Capital Stock* ACCOUNT NO. *31*

DATE		ITEM	POST. REF.	DEBIT	CREDIT	BALANCE	
						DEBIT	CREDIT

ACCOUNT *Retained Earnings* ACCOUNT NO. *32*

DATE		ITEM	POST. REF.	DEBIT	CREDIT	BALANCE	
						DEBIT	CREDIT

PROBLEM 4-5 ___, Continued

ACCOUNT *Dividends* ACCOUNT NO. *33*

DATE		ITEM	POST. REF.	DEBIT	CREDIT	BALANCE	
						DEBIT	CREDIT

ACCOUNT *Income Summary* ACCOUNT NO. *34*

DATE		ITEM	POST. REF.	DEBIT	CREDIT	BALANCE	
						DEBIT	CREDIT

ACCOUNT *Service Revenue* ACCOUNT NO. *41*

DATE		ITEM	POST. REF.	DEBIT	CREDIT	BALANCE	
						DEBIT	CREDIT

ACCOUNT *Wages Expense* ACCOUNT NO. *51*

DATE		ITEM	POST. REF.	DEBIT	CREDIT	BALANCE	
						DEBIT	CREDIT

ACCOUNT *Supplies Expense* ACCOUNT NO. *52*

DATE		ITEM	POST. REF.	DEBIT	CREDIT	BALANCE	
						DEBIT	CREDIT

PROBLEM 4-5 ___, Continued

ACCOUNT *Rent Expense* ACCOUNT NO. *53*

DATE	ITEM	POST. REF.	DEBIT	CREDIT	BALANCE	
					DEBIT	CREDIT

ACCOUNT *Depreciation Expense—Equipment* ACCOUNT NO. *54*

DATE	ITEM	POST. REF.	DEBIT	CREDIT	BALANCE	
					DEBIT	CREDIT

ACCOUNT *Truck Expense* ACCOUNT NO. *55*

DATE	ITEM	POST. REF.	DEBIT	CREDIT	BALANCE	
					DEBIT	CREDIT

ACCOUNT *Depreciation Expense—Trucks* ACCOUNT NO. *56*

DATE	ITEM	POST. REF.	DEBIT	CREDIT	BALANCE	
					DEBIT	CREDIT

ACCOUNT *Insurance Expense* ACCOUNT NO. *57*

DATE	ITEM	POST. REF.	DEBIT	CREDIT	BALANCE	
					DEBIT	CREDIT

PROBLEM 4-5 ___, Continued

ACCOUNT *Miscellaneous Expense* ACCOUNT NO. *59*

DATE		ITEM	POST. REF.	DEBIT	CREDIT	BALANCE DEBIT	BALANCE CREDIT

3.

JOURNAL PAGE *26*

	DATE		DESCRIPTION	POST. REF.	DEBIT	CREDIT	
1			*Adjusting Entries*				1
2							2
3							3
4							4
5							5
6							6
7							7
8							8
9							9
10							10
11							11
12							12
13							13
14							14
15							15
16							16
17							17
18							18
19							19
20							20
21							21
22							22
23							23
24							24
25							25
26							26
27							27
28							28

PROBLEM 4-5 ___, Continued

4. *Omit "00" in the cents columns.*

Adjusted Trial Balance

PROBLEM 4-5 ___, Continued

5. *Omit "00" in the cents columns.*

Income Statement

Retained Earnings Statement

PROBLEM 4-5 ___, Continued

Balance Sheet

PROBLEM 4-5 ___, Concluded

6.

JOURNAL PAGE *27*

DATE		DESCRIPTION	POST. REF.	DEBIT	CREDIT
		Closing Entries			

7.

Post-Closing Trial Balance

Page not used.

Page not used.

CONTINUING PROBLEM

1.

	ACCOUNT TITLE	TRIAL BALANCE		ADJUSTMENTS		
		DEBIT	CREDIT	DEBIT	CREDIT	
1						1
2						2
3						3
4						4
5						5
6						6
7						7
8						8
9						9
10						10
11						11
12						12
13						13
14						14
15						15
16						16
17						17
18						18
19						19
20						20
21						21
22						22
23						23
24						24
25						25
26						26
27						27
28						28
29						29
30						30
31						31
32						32
33						33
34						34

CONTINUING PROBLEM, Continued

	ADJUSTED TRIAL BALANCE		INCOME STATEMENT		BALANCE SHEET		
	DEBIT	CREDIT	DEBIT	CREDIT	DEBIT	CREDIT	
1							1
2							2
3							3
4							4
5							5
6							6
7							7
8							8
9							9
10							10
11							11
12							12
13							13
14							14
15							15
16							16
17							17
18							18
19							19
20							20
21							21
22							22
23							23
24							24
25							25
26							26
27							27
28							28
29							29
30							30
31							31
32							32
33							33
34							34

Page not used.

CONTINUING PROBLEM, Continued

2.

Income Statement

Retained Earnings Statement

CONTINUING PROBLEM, Continued

Balance Sheet

CONTINUING PROBLEM, Continued

3. Note: Use the general ledger accounts provided in Chapter 2, pages 78–83.

JOURNAL

PAGE *4*

DATE		DESCRIPTION	POST. REF.	DEBIT	CREDIT
		Closing Entries			

CONTINUING PROBLEM, Concluded

4.

EXERCISE 5-1

a. ______________________________

b. ______________________________

c. ______________________________

____

____

EXERCISE 5-2

____

EXERCISE 5-3

a. Purchases – (X + X) = Net purchases

____

b. Net purchases + X = Cost of merchandise purchased

____

c. Merchandise inventory (beginning) + Cost of merchandise purchased = X

____

d. Merchandise available for sale – X = Cost of merchandise sold

____

EXERCISE 5-4

a. ______________________________

b. ______________________________

EXERCISE 5-5

EXERCISE 5-6

Net sales: ______

Gross profit: ______

EXERCISE 5-7

1. Advertising expense: ______
2. Depreciation expense on office equipment: ______
3. Insurance expense on store equipment: ______
4. Interest expense on notes payable: ______
5. Office supplies used: ______
6. Rent expense on office building: ______
7. Salaries of office personnel: ______
8. Salary of sales manager: ______

EXERCISE 5-15

(1) ______________________

(2) ______________________

(3) ______________________

(4) ______________________

(5) ______________________

EXERCISE 5-16

a. Amount of the sale: ______________________

b. Amount debited to Accounts Receivable: ______________________

c. Amount of the discount for early payment: ______________________

d. Amount due within the discount period: ______________________

EXERCISE 5-17

a. ______________________

b. ______________________

EXERCISE 5-18

EXERCISE 5-19

(1)

(2)

(3)

(4)

EXERCISE 5-20

a.–c.

JOURNAL PAGE

	DATE		DESCRIPTION	POST. REF.	DEBIT	CREDIT	
1							1
2							2
3							3
4							4
5							5
6							6
7							7
8							8
9							9
10							10

EXERCISE 5-21

a.–e.

JOURNAL PAGE

	DATE		DESCRIPTION	POST. REF.	DEBIT	CREDIT	
1							1
2							2
3							3
4							4
5							5
6							6
7							7
8							8
9							9
10							10
11							11
12							12
13							13
14							14
15							15
16							16
17							17
18							18

EXERCISE 5-22

	Merchandise	Transportation Paid by Seller		Returns and Allowances	Amount to be Paid in Full
a.	$12,000	—	FOB destination, n/30	$1,500	$ ________
b.	4,500	$200	FOB shipping point, 1/10, n/30	500	$ ________
c.	5,000	—	FOB shipping point, 2/10, n/30	—	$ ________
d.	5,000	—	FOB shipping point, 1/10, n/30	1,000	$ ________
e.	1,500	50	FOB destination, 2/10, n/30	700	$ ________

EXERCISE 5-23

a. ______________________________

b. ______________________________

c. ______________________________

d. ______________________________

EXERCISE 5-24

a. and b.

JOURNAL PAGE

	DATE	DESCRIPTION	POST. REF.	DEBIT	CREDIT	
1						1
2						2
3						3
4						4
5						5
6						6
7						7
8						8
9						9
10						10
11						11
12						12

EXERCISE 5-25

a.–c.

JOURNAL PAGE

	DATE	DESCRIPTION	POST. REF.	DEBIT	CREDIT	
1						1
2						2
3						3
4						4
5						5
6						6
7						7
8						8
9						9
10						10
11						11
12						12
13						13
14						14
15						15
16						16
17						17
18						18

EXERCISE 5-26

a.–c.

JOURNAL PAGE

	DATE		DESCRIPTION	POST. REF.	DEBIT	CREDIT	
1							1
2							2
3							3
4							4
5							5
6							6
7							7
8							8
9							9
10							10
11							11
12							12
13							13
14							14

EXERCISE 5-27

	Debit	Credit
a. Cost of Merchandise Sold	________	________
b. Merchandise Inventory	________	________
c. Sales	________	________
d. Sales Discounts	________	________
e. Sales Returns and Allowances	________	________
f. Transportation Out	________	________

EXERCISE 5-28

Balance Sheet Accounts

Acct #	Account Name

Income Statement Accounts

Acct #	Account Name

EXERCISE 5-29

JOURNAL PAGE

	DATE		DESCRIPTION	POST. REF.	DEBIT	CREDIT	
1							1
2							2
3							3
4							4
5							5

EXERCISE 5-30

(a) Accounts Receivable: ____________________

(b) Cost of Merchandise Sold: ____________________

(c) Merchandise Inventory: ____________________

(d) Sales: ____________________

(e) Sales Discounts: ____________________

(f) Sales Returns and Allowances: ____________________

(g) Salaries Expense: ____________________

(h) Salaries Payable: ____________________

(i) Supplies: ____________________

(j) Supplies Expense: ____________________

EXERCISE 5-31

a. 2003: ____________________

2002: ____________________

b. ____________________

EXERCISE 5-32

a. ______________________________

b. ______________________________

APPENDIX EXERCISE 5-33

JOURNAL PAGE

	DATE		DESCRIPTION	POST. REF.	DEBIT	CREDIT	
1							1
2							2
3							3
4							4
5							5
6							6
7							7
8							8
9							9
10							10
11							11
12							12
13							13
14							14
15							15
16							16
17							17
18							18
19							19
20							20
21							21

PROBLEM 5-1 ___

1. *Omit "00" in the cents columns.*

PROBLEM 5-1 ___, Continued

2. *Omit "00" in the cents columns.*

Name ____________________________________

PROBLEM 5-1 ___, Continued

3. *Omit "00" in the cents columns.*

PROBLEM 5-1 ___, Concluded

4. a. ______________________________

b. ______________________________

PROBLEM 5-2 ___

1. *Omit "00" in the cents columns.*

2. *Omit "00" in the cents columns.*

PROBLEM 5-2 ___, Continued

3. *Omit "00" in the cents columns.*

Balance

PROBLEM 5-2 ___, Concluded

Sheet

Page not used.

Name ______________________________________

PROBLEM 5-3 ___

JOURNAL

PAGE

DATE		DESCRIPTION	POST. REF.	DEBIT	CREDIT

PROBLEM 5-3 ___, Continued

JOURNAL

PAGE

DATE		DESCRIPTION	POST. REF.	DEBIT	CREDIT

PROBLEM 5-3 ___, Continued

JOURNAL

PAGE

DATE		DESCRIPTION	POST. REF.	DEBIT	CREDIT

PROBLEM 5-3 ___, Concluded

JOURNAL

PAGE

DATE		DESCRIPTION	POST. REF.	DEBIT	CREDIT

PROBLEM 5-4 ___

JOURNAL

PAGE

DATE		DESCRIPTION	POST. REF.	DEBIT	CREDIT

PROBLEM 5-4 ___, Concluded

JOURNAL

PAGE

DATE		DESCRIPTION	POST. REF.	DEBIT	CREDIT

PROBLEM 5-5 ___

JOURNAL PAGE

DATE		DESCRIPTION	POST. REF.	DEBIT	CREDIT

PROBLEM 5-5 ___, Concluded

JOURNAL

PAGE

DATE		DESCRIPTION	POST. REF.	DEBIT	CREDIT

Page not used.

APPENDIX PROBLEM 5-7 ___

1.

ACCOUNT TITLE	TRIAL BALANCE		ADJUSTMENTS	
	DEBIT	CREDIT	DEBIT	CREDIT

Name ____

APPENDIX PROBLEM 5-7 ___, Continued

____

____

____

	ADJUSTED TRIAL BALANCE		INCOME STATEMENT		BALANCE SHEET		
	DEBIT	CREDIT	DEBIT	CREDIT	DEBIT	CREDIT	
1							1
2							2
3							3
4							4
5							5
6							6
7							7
8							8
9							9
10							10
11							11
12							12
13							13
14							14
15							15
16							16
17							17
18							18
19							19
20							20
21							21
22							22
23							23
24							24
25							25
26							26
27							27
28							28
29							29
30							30
31							31
32							32
33							33
34							34
35							35
36							36
37							37

Page not used.

Name ____

APPENDIX PROBLEM 5-7 ___, Continued

2. *Omit "00" in the cents columns.*

APPENDIX PROBLEM 5-7 ___, Continued

3. *Omit "00" in the cents columns.*

APPENDIX PROBLEM 5-7 ___, Continued

4. *Omit "00" in the cents columns.*

APPENDIX PROBLEM 5-7 ___, Continued

5.

JOURNAL

PAGE

	DATE		DESCRIPTION	POST. REF.	DEBIT	CREDIT	
1							1
2							2
3							3
4							4
5							5
6							6
7							7
8							8
9							9
10							10
11							11
12							12
13							13
14							14
15							15
16							16
17							17
18							18
19							19
20							20
21							21
22							22
23							23
24							24
25							25
26							26
27							27
28							28
29							29
30							30
31							31
32							32
33							33
34							34
35							35
36							36

APPENDIX PROBLEM 5-7 ___, Concluded

6.

JOURNAL

PAGE

DATE		DESCRIPTION	POST. REF.	DEBIT	CREDIT

Page not used.

Name ____________________

COMPREHENSIVE PROBLEM 2

2., 4., and 6., or alt. 2., 6., and 7.

JOURNAL

PAGE *20*

	DATE		DESCRIPTION	POST. REF.	DEBIT	CREDIT	
1							1
2							2
3							3
4							4
5							5
6							6
7							7
8							8
9							9
10							10
11							11
12							12
13							13
14							14
15							15
16							16
17							17
18							18
19							19
20							20
21							21
22							22
23							23
24							24
25							25
26							26
27							27
28							28
29							29
30							30
31							31
32							32
33							33
34							34
35							35
36							36

COMPREHENSIVE PROBLEM 2, Continued

JOURNAL

PAGE *21*

DATE		DESCRIPTION	POST. REF.	DEBIT	CREDIT

COMPREHENSIVE PROBLEM 2, Continued

JOURNAL

PAGE *22*

DATE	DESCRIPTION	POST. REF.	DEBIT	CREDIT

COMPREHENSIVE PROBLEM 2, Continued

JOURNAL

PAGE *23*

DATE		DESCRIPTION	POST. REF.	DEBIT	CREDIT

COMPREHENSIVE PROBLEM 2, Continued

JOURNAL

PAGE *24*

DATE		DESCRIPTION	POST. REF.	DEBIT	CREDIT

COMPREHENSIVE PROBLEM 2, Continued

1., 3., 4., and 6., or alt. 1., 3., 6., and 7.

ACCOUNT *Cash* ACCOUNT NO. *110*

DATE		ITEM	POST. REF.	DEBIT	CREDIT	BALANCE	
						DEBIT	CREDIT

COMPREHENSIVE PROBLEM 2, Continued

ACCOUNT *Accounts Receivable* ACCOUNT NO. *112*

DATE	ITEM	POST. REF.	DEBIT	CREDIT	BALANCE	
					DEBIT	CREDIT

ACCOUNT *Merchandise Inventory* ACCOUNT NO. *115*

DATE	ITEM	POST. REF.	DEBIT	CREDIT	BALANCE	
					DEBIT	CREDIT

COMPREHENSIVE PROBLEM 2, Continued

ACCOUNT *Prepaid Insurance* ACCOUNT NO. *116*

DATE		ITEM	POST. REF.	DEBIT	CREDIT	BALANCE	
						DEBIT	CREDIT

ACCOUNT *Store Supplies* ACCOUNT NO. *117*

DATE		ITEM	POST. REF.	DEBIT	CREDIT	BALANCE	
						DEBIT	CREDIT

ACCOUNT *Store Equipment* ACCOUNT NO. *123*

DATE		ITEM	POST. REF.	DEBIT	CREDIT	BALANCE	
						DEBIT	CREDIT

ACCOUNT *Accumulated Depreciation—Store Equipment* ACCOUNT NO. *124*

DATE		ITEM	POST. REF.	DEBIT	CREDIT	BALANCE	
						DEBIT	CREDIT

COMPREHENSIVE PROBLEM 2, Continued

ACCOUNT *Accounts Payable* ACCOUNT NO. *210*

DATE		ITEM	POST. REF.	DEBIT	CREDIT	BALANCE	
						DEBIT	CREDIT

ACCOUNT *Salaries Payable* ACCOUNT NO. *211*

DATE		ITEM	POST. REF.	DEBIT	CREDIT	BALANCE	
						DEBIT	CREDIT

ACCOUNT *Capital Stock* ACCOUNT NO. *310*

DATE		ITEM	POST. REF.	DEBIT	CREDIT	BALANCE	
						DEBIT	CREDIT

ACCOUNT *Retained Earnings* ACCOUNT NO. *311*

DATE		ITEM	POST. REF.	DEBIT	CREDIT	BALANCE	
						DEBIT	CREDIT

COMPREHENSIVE PROBLEM 2, Continued

ACCOUNT *Dividends* ACCOUNT NO. *312*

DATE		ITEM	POST. REF.	DEBIT	CREDIT	BALANCE DEBIT	BALANCE CREDIT

ACCOUNT *Income Summary* ACCOUNT NO. *313*

DATE		ITEM	POST. REF.	DEBIT	CREDIT	BALANCE DEBIT	BALANCE CREDIT

ACCOUNT *Sales* ACCOUNT NO. *410*

DATE		ITEM	POST. REF.	DEBIT	CREDIT	BALANCE DEBIT	BALANCE CREDIT

ACCOUNT *Sales Returns and Allowances* ACCOUNT NO. *411*

DATE		ITEM	POST. REF.	DEBIT	CREDIT	BALANCE DEBIT	BALANCE CREDIT

COMPREHENSIVE PROBLEM 2, Continued

ACCOUNT *Sales Discounts* ACCOUNT NO. *412*

DATE	ITEM	POST. REF.	DEBIT	CREDIT	BALANCE DEBIT	BALANCE CREDIT

ACCOUNT *Cost of Merchandise Sold* ACCOUNT NO. *510*

DATE	ITEM	POST. REF.	DEBIT	CREDIT	BALANCE DEBIT	BALANCE CREDIT

ACCOUNT *Sales Salaries Expense* ACCOUNT NO. *520*

DATE	ITEM	POST. REF.	DEBIT	CREDIT	BALANCE DEBIT	BALANCE CREDIT

COMPREHENSIVE PROBLEM 2, Continued

ACCOUNT *Advertising Expense* ACCOUNT NO. *521*

DATE		ITEM	POST. REF.	DEBIT	CREDIT	BALANCE DEBIT	BALANCE CREDIT

ACCOUNT *Depreciation Expense* ACCOUNT NO. *522*

DATE		ITEM	POST. REF.	DEBIT	CREDIT	BALANCE DEBIT	BALANCE CREDIT

ACCOUNT *Store Supplies Expense* ACCOUNT NO. *523*

DATE		ITEM	POST. REF.	DEBIT	CREDIT	BALANCE DEBIT	BALANCE CREDIT

ACCOUNT *Miscellaneous Selling Expense* ACCOUNT NO. *529*

DATE		ITEM	POST. REF.	DEBIT	CREDIT	BALANCE DEBIT	BALANCE CREDIT

Name ____

COMPREHENSIVE PROBLEM 2, Continued

ACCOUNT *Office Salaries Expense* ACCOUNT NO. *530*

DATE		ITEM	POST. REF.	DEBIT	CREDIT	BALANCE	
						DEBIT	CREDIT

ACCOUNT *Rent Expense* ACCOUNT NO. *531*

DATE		ITEM	POST. REF.	DEBIT	CREDIT	BALANCE	
						DEBIT	CREDIT

ACCOUNT *Insurance Expense* ACCOUNT NO. *532*

DATE		ITEM	POST. REF.	DEBIT	CREDIT	BALANCE	
						DEBIT	CREDIT

ACCOUNT *Miscellaneous Administrative Expense* ACCOUNT NO. *539*

DATE		ITEM	POST. REF.	DEBIT	CREDIT	BALANCE	
						DEBIT	CREDIT

COMPREHENSIVE PROBLEM 2, Continued

alt. 4. *This work sheet is applicable only if following alternative instructions.*

	ACCOUNT TITLE	TRIAL BALANCE		ADJUSTMENTS		
		DEBIT	CREDIT	DEBIT	CREDIT	
1						1
2						2
3						3
4						4
5						5
6						6
7						7
8						8
9						9
10						10
11						11
12						12
13						13
14						14
15						15
16						16
17						17
18						18
19						19
20						20
21						21
22						22
23						23
24						24
25						25
26						26
27						27
28						28
29						29
30						30
31						31
32						32
33						33
34						34

COMPREHENSIVE PROBLEM 2, Continued

	ADJUSTED TRIAL BALANCE		INCOME STATEMENT		BALANCE SHEET		
	DEBIT	CREDIT	DEBIT	CREDIT	DEBIT	CREDIT	
1							1
2							2
3							3
4							4
5							5
6							6
7							7
8							8
9							9
10							10
11							11
12							12
13							13
14							14
15							15
16							16
17							17
18							18
19							19
20							20
21							21
22							22
23							23
24							24
25							25
26							26
27							27
28							28
29							29
30							30
31							31
32							32
33							33
34							34

Page not used.

COMPREHENSIVE PROBLEM 2, Continued

5. or alt. 5. *Omit "00" in the cents columns.*

Income Statement

COMPREHENSIVE PROBLEM 2, Continued

Omit "00" in the cents columns.

Retained Earnings Statement

COMPREHENSIVE PROBLEM 2, Continued

Omit "00" in the cents columns.

Balance Sheet

COMPREHENSIVE PROBLEM 2, Concluded

7. or alt. 8. *Omit "00" in the cents columns.*

Post-Closing Trial Balance

EXERCISE 6-1

a.–c.

EXERCISE 6-2

a.

EXERCISE 6-2, Concluded

b. 1.–3.

EXERCISE 6-3

EXERCISE 6-4

EXERCISE 6-5

EXERCISE 6-6

Name ______________________________

EXERCISE 6-7

a. ______________________________

b. ______________________________

EXERCISE 6-8

a. ______________________________

b. ______________________________

EXERCISE 6-9

EXERCISE 6-10

a.

b.

EXERCISE 6-11

JOURNAL PAGE

	DATE		DESCRIPTION	POST. REF.	DEBIT	CREDIT	
1							1
2							2
3							3
4							4
5							5

Name ______________________________

EXERCISE 6-12

JOURNAL PAGE

	DATE		DESCRIPTION	POST. REF.	DEBIT	CREDIT	
1							1
2							2
3							3
4							4
5							5

EXERCISE 6-13

EXERCISE 6-14

EXERCISE 6-15

1.
2.
3.
4.
5.
6.
7.

EXERCISE 6-16

1.
2.
3.
4.
5.
6.
7.

Name ____________________

EXERCISE 6-17

EXERCISE 6-18

JOURNAL PAGE

	DATE		DESCRIPTION	POST. REF.	DEBIT	CREDIT	
1							1
2							2
3							3
4							4
5							5

EXERCISE 6-19

JOURNAL PAGE

	DATE		DESCRIPTION	POST. REF.	DEBIT	CREDIT	
1							1
2							2
3							3
4							4

EXERCISE 6-20

a.

b. ____________________

EXERCISE 6-21

EXERCISE 6-21, Concluded

EXERCISE 6-22

a.

b.

EXERCISE 6-22, Concluded

EXERCISE 6-23

a. and b.

JOURNAL PAGE

	DATE		DESCRIPTION	POST. REF.	DEBIT	CREDIT	
1							1
2							2
3							3
4							4
5							5
6							6
7							7
8							8

EXERCISE 6-24

EXERCISE 6-25

a. 2003:

2002:

b.

Name ____

PROBLEM 6-1 ___

PROBLEM 6-1 ___, Concluded

PROBLEM 6-2 ___

JOURNAL

PAGE

	DATE		DESCRIPTION	POST. REF.	DEBIT	CREDIT	
1							1
2							2
3							3
4							4
5							5
6							6
7							7
8							8
9							9
10							10
11							11
12							12
13							13
14							14
15							15
16							16
17							17
18							18
19							19
20							20
21							21
22							22
23							23
24							24
25							25
26							26
27							27
28							28
29							29
30							30
31							31
32							32
33							33
34							34
35							35
36							36

PROBLEM 6-2 ___, Concluded

JOURNAL

PAGE

DATE		DESCRIPTION	POST. REF.	DEBIT	CREDIT

Name ______________________________________

PROBLEM 6-3 ___

1.

PROBLEM 6-3 ___, Concluded

2.

JOURNAL

PAGE

	DATE	DESCRIPTION	POST. REF.	DEBIT	CREDIT	
1						1
2						2
3						3
4						4
5						5
6						6
7						7
8						8
9						9
10						10
11						11
12						12
13						13
14						14
15						15
16						16
17						17
18						18
19						19
20						20
21						21
22						22
23						23
24						24
25						25
26						26
27						27
28						28
29						29
30						30
31						31
32						32
33						33
34						34
35						35
36						36

Name ____

PROBLEM 6-4 ___

1.

PROBLEM 6-4 ___, Concluded

2.

JOURNAL

PAGE

DATE		DESCRIPTION	POST. REF.	DEBIT	CREDIT

PROBLEM 6-5 ___

1.

PROBLEM 6-5 ___, Concluded

2.

JOURNAL PAGE

	DATE		DESCRIPTION	POST. REF.	DEBIT	CREDIT	
1							1
2							2
3							3
4							4
5							5
6							6
7							7
8							8
9							9
10							10
11							11
12							12
13							13
14							14
15							15
16							16
17							17
18							18
19							19
20							20
21							21
22							22
23							23
24							24

3. $ ______________________________

4. ______________________________

EXERCISE 7-1

a.–e.

EXERCISE 7-2

a. ______________________________

____

____

b. ______________________________

____

____

c. ______________________________

____

____

____

____

____

____

____

EXERCISE 7-3

Account	Due Date	Number of Days Past Due
Bear Creek Body Shop	June 8	
First Auto	July 3	
Kaiser Repair	March 20	
Master's Auto Repair	May 15	
Richter Auto	June 18	
Sabol's	April 12	
Uptown Auto	May 8	
Westside Repair & Tow	May 31	

EXERCISE 7-4

a.

Customer	Due Date	Number of Days Past Due
Janzen Industries	August 29	
Kuehn Company	September 3	
Mauer Inc.	October 21	
Pollack Company	November 23	
Simrill Company	December 3	

EXERCISE 7-4, Concluded

b.

Aging of Accounts Receivable

November 30

CUSTOMER	BALANCE	NOT PAST DUE	DAYS PAST DUE			
			1–30	31–60	61–90	OVER 90
Aaker Brothers Inc.	*2000*	*2000*				
Aitken Company	*1500*		*1500*			
~	~	~	~	~	~	~
Zollo Company	*5000*			*5000*		
Subtotals	*972500*	*640000*	*180000*	*78500*	*42300*	*31700*

EXERCISE 7-5

	BALANCE	NOT PAST DUE	DAYS PAST DUE			
			1–30	31–60	61–90	OVER 90

EXERCISE 7-6

JOURNAL PAGE

	DATE		DESCRIPTION	POST. REF.	DEBIT	CREDIT	
1							1
2							2
3							3
4							4
5							5

EXERCISE 7-7

		Estimated Uncollectible Accounts	
Age Interval	**Balance**	**Percent**	**Amount**
Not past due	$450,000	2%	$
1–30 days past due	110,000	4	
31–60 days past due	51,000	6	
61–90 days past due	1,500	20	
91–180 days past due	7,500	60	
Over 180 days past due	5,500	80	
Total	$636,500		$

EXERCISE 7-8

JOURNAL PAGE

	DATE		DESCRIPTION	POST. REF.	DEBIT	CREDIT	
1							1
2							2
3							3
4							4
5							5

EXERCISE 7-9

a. ____________________

b. ____________________

c. ____________________

d. ____________________

EXERCISE 7-10

a.–b.

JOURNAL

PAGE

	DATE	DESCRIPTION	POST. REF.	DEBIT	CREDIT	
1						1
2						2
3						3
4						4
5						5
6						6
7						7
8						8
9						9
10						10

EXERCISE 7-11

JOURNAL

PAGE

	DATE	DESCRIPTION	POST. REF.	DEBIT	CREDIT	
1						1
2						2
3						3
4						4
5						5
6						6
7						7
8						8
9						9
10						10
11						11
12						12
13						13
14						14
15						15
16						16
17						17
18						18
19						19
20						20

EXERCISE 7-12

JOURNAL PAGE

	DATE		DESCRIPTION	POST. REF.	DEBIT	CREDIT	
1							1
2							2
3							3
4							4
5							5
6							6
7							7
8							8
9							9
10							10
11							11
12							12
13							13
14							14
15							15

EXERCISE 7-13

____

____

EXERCISE 7-14

a. ____

b. ____

EXERCISE 7-15

	Date of Note	Face Amount	Term of Note	Interest Rate	Due Date	Interest Due
a.	June2	$ 8,000	90 days	6%	________	$________
b.	August 30	18,000	120 days	8%	________	$________
c.	October 1	12,500	60 days	12%	________	$________
d.	March 6	10,000	60 days	9%	________	$________
e.	May 20	6,000	60 days	10%	________	$________

EXERCISE 7-16

a. ____

b. ____

EXERCISE 7-16, Concluded

c. (1) and (2)

JOURNAL PAGE

	DATE		DESCRIPTION	POST. REF.	DEBIT	CREDIT	
1							1
2							2
3							3
4							4
5							5
6							6

EXERCISE 7-17

1. ______________________________
2. ______________________________
3. ______________________________
4. ______________________________
5. ______________________________
6. ______________________________
7. ______________________________

EXERCISE 7-18

JOURNAL PAGE

	DATE		DESCRIPTION	POST. REF.	DEBIT	CREDIT	
1							1
2							2
3							3
4							4
5							5
6							6
7							7
8							8
9							9
10							10
11							11
12							12
13							13
14							14
15							15

EXERCISE 7-19

JOURNAL PAGE

	DATE		DESCRIPTION	POST. REF.	DEBIT	CREDIT	
1							1
2							2
3							3
4							4
5							5
6							6
7							7
8							8
9							9
10							10
11							11
12							12
13							13
14							14

EXERCISE 7-20

JOURNAL PAGE

	DATE		DESCRIPTION	POST. REF.	DEBIT	CREDIT	
1							1
2							2
3							3
4							4
5							5
6							6
7							7
8							8
9							9
10							10
11							11
12							12
13							13
14							14
15							15
16							16
17							17

Name ___________________________________

EXERCISE 7-20, Concluded

JOURNAL PAGE

	DATE		DESCRIPTION	POST. REF.	DEBIT	CREDIT	
1							1
2							2
3							3
4							4
5							5
6							6
7							7
8							8
9							9
10							10

EXERCISE 7-21

EXERCISE 7-22

a. 2003: ___________________________________

2002: ___________________________________

b. ___________________________________

EXERCISE 7-23

a. 2002: ____________________

2001: ____________________

b. ____________________

EXERCISE 7-24

a. 2002: ____________________

2001: ____________________

b. 2002: ____________________

2001: ____________________

c. ____________________

APPENDIX EXERCISE 7-25

a. ______________________

b. ______________________

c. ______________________

d. ______________________

e.

JOURNAL PAGE

	DATE		DESCRIPTION	POST. REF.	DEBIT	CREDIT	
1							1
2							2
3							3
4							4

APPENDIX EXERCISE 7-26

JOURNAL PAGE

	DATE		DESCRIPTION	POST. REF.	DEBIT	CREDIT	
1							1
2							2
3							3
4							4
5							5
6							6
7							7
8							8
9							9
10							10
11							11
12							12
13							13
14							14
15							15
16							16
17							17
18							18
19							19
20							20
21							21
22							22

Page not used.

Name ______________________________

PROBLEM 7-2 ___

1.

Customer	Due Date	Number of Days Past Due

2. and 3. *The aging-of-receivables schedule is on page 298.*

4.

JOURNAL PAGE

	DATE		DESCRIPTION	POST. REF.	DEBIT	CREDIT	
1							1
2							2
3							3
4							4
5							5
6							6
7							7
8							8
9							9
10							10
11							11
12							12
13							13
14							14

PROBLEM 7-2 ___, Concluded

2. and 3.

Aging of Accounts Receivable

December 31, 2006

CUSTOMER	BALANCE	NOT PAST DUE	DAYS PAST DUE				
			1–30	31–60	61–90	91–120	OVER 120

Name ______________________________

PROBLEM 7-3 ___

1.

Year	Uncollectible Accounts Expense			Balance of Allowance Account, End of Year
	Expense Actually Reported	Expense Based on Estimate	Increase (Decrease) in Amount of Expense	

2.

PROBLEM 7-3 ___, Concluded

PROBLEM 7-4 ___

1.

Note	(a) Due Date	(b) Interest Due at Maturity
(1)		
(2)		
(3)		
(4)		
(5)		
(6)		

2. and 3.

JOURNAL

PAGE

DATE		DESCRIPTION	POST. REF.	DEBIT	CREDIT

PROBLEM 7-4 ___, Concluded

4.

JOURNAL PAGE

	DATE		DESCRIPTION	POST. REF.	DEBIT	CREDIT	
1							1
2							2
3							3
4							4
5							5
6							6
7							7
8							8
9							9
10							10
11							11
12							12
13							13
14							14
15							15
16							16
17							17
18							18
19							19
20							20
21							21
22							22
23							23
24							24
25							25
26							26
27							27
28							28
29							29
30							30
31							31
32							32
33							33
34							34
35							35
36							36

Name ______________________________

PROBLEM 7-5 ___

JOURNAL

PAGE

DATE		DESCRIPTION	POST. REF.	DEBIT	CREDIT

PROBLEM 7-5 ___, Concluded

JOURNAL

PAGE

DATE		DESCRIPTION	POST. REF.	DEBIT	CREDIT

Name ______________________________________

PROBLEM 7-6 ___

JOURNAL

PAGE

	DATE		DESCRIPTION	POST. REF.	DEBIT	CREDIT	
1							1
2							2
3							3
4							4
5							5
6							6
7							7
8							8
9							9
10							10
11							11
12							12
13							13
14							14
15							15
16							16
17							17
18							18
19							19
20							20
21							21
22							22
23							23
24							24
25							25
26							26
27							27
28							28
29							29
30							30
31							31
32							32
33							33
34							34
35							35
36							36

PROBLEM 7-6 ___, Concluded

JOURNAL

PAGE

DATE		DESCRIPTION	POST. REF.	DEBIT	CREDIT

EXERCISE 8-1

EXERCISE 8-2

a.

b.

c.

EXERCISE 8-3

a. ______ f. ______

b. ______ g. ______

c. ______ h. ______

d. ______ i. ______

e. ______

EXERCISE 8-4

a. **Balance Sheet**

Merchandise inventory .... ____________________

Current assets .... ____________________

Total assets .... ____________________

Total stockholders' equity (retained earnings) .... ____________________

b. **Income Statement**

Cost of merchandise sold .... ____________________

Gross profit .... ____________________

Net income .... ____________________

EXERCISE 8-5

a. **Balance Sheet**

Merchandise inventory .... ____________________

Current assets .... ____________________

Total assets .... ____________________

Total stockholders' equity (retained earnings) .... ____________________

b. **Income Statement**

Cost of merchandise sold .... ____________________

Gross profit .... ____________________

Net income .... ____________________

EXERCISE 8-6

EXERCISE 8-9

Cell Phones									
Date	Purchases			Cost of Merchandise Sold			Inventory		
	Quantity	Unit Cost	Total Cost	Quantity	Unit Cost	Total Cost	Quantity	Unit Cost	Total Cost

Total cost of merchandise sold: ______________________

Inventory, March 31: ______________________

EXERCISE 8-10

Cell Phones									
	Purchases			Cost of Merchandise Sold			Inventory		
Date	Quantity	Unit Cost	Total Cost	Quantity	Unit Cost	Total Cost	Quantity	Unit Cost	Total Cost

Total cost of merchandise sold: ______________________________

Inventory, October 31: ______________________________

EXERCISE 8-11

a. Fifo: ____________________

b. Lifo: ____________________

EXERCISE 8-12

a. First-in, first-out method: ____________________

b. Last-in, first-out method: ____________________

c. Average cost method: ____________________

EXERCISE 8-13

	Cost	
Inventory Method	**Merchandise Inventory**	**Merchandise Sold**
a. First-in, first-out		
b. Last-in, first-out................		
c. Average cost		

Supporting calculations:

EXERCISE 8-13, Concluded

EXERCISE 8-14

1. a.
   b.
   c.
   d.
2.

EXERCISE 8-15

Commodity	Inventory Quantity	Unit Cost Price	Unit Market Price	Total Cost	Total Market	Total Lower of C or M
M76	8	$150	$160	$	$	$
T53	20	75	70			
A19	10	275	260			
J81	15	50	40			
K10	25	101	105			
Total				$	$	$

EXERCISE 8-16

EXERCISE 8-17

EXERCISE 8-18

	COST	RETAIL

EXERCISE 8-19

a.

b.

EXERCISE 8-20

a. Apple Computer: ____________________

American Greetings: ____________________

b. ____________________

EXERCISE 8-21

a. ____________________

EXERCISE 8-21, Concluded

b._____

c.

PROBLEM 8-1 ___

1.

Date	Purchases			Cost of Merchandise Sold			Inventory		
	Quantity	Unit Cost	Total Cost	Quantity	Unit Cost	Total Cost	Quantity	Unit Cost	Total Cost

Total cost of merchandise sold .... ________

PROBLEM 8-1 ___, Concluded

2.

JOURNAL PAGE

	DATE		DESCRIPTION	POST. REF.	DEBIT	CREDIT	
1							1
2							2
3							3
4							4
5							5
6							6
7							7
8							8
9							9
10							10
11							11
12							12
13							13
14							14
15							15
16							16
17							17
18							18
19							19
20							20
21							21
22							22
23							23
24							24
25							25
26							26
27							27
28							28
29							29
30							30
31							31
32							32

3. $ ______________________________

4. $ ______________________________

PROBLEM 8-2 ___

1.

Date	Purchases			Cost of Merchandise Sold			Inventory		
	Quantity	Unit Cost	Total Cost	Quantity	Unit Cost	Total Cost	Quantity	Unit Cost	Total Cost

Total cost of merchandise sold .... ______

PROBLEM 8-2 ___, Concluded

2. and 3.

Name ______________________________

PROBLEM 8-3 ___

1. **FIRST-IN, FIRST-OUT METHOD**

Model	Quantity	Unit Cost	Total Cost

2. **LAST-IN, FIRST-OUT METHOD**

Model	Quantity	Unit Cost	Total Cost

PROBLEM 8-3 ___, Concluded

3. **AVERAGE COST METHOD**

Model	Quantity	Unit Cost	Total Cost

4. a. ______________________________

b. ______________________________

PROBLEM 8-4 ___

Inventory Sheet

December 31, 2006

Description	Inventory Quantity	Unit Cost Price	Unit Market Price	Total Cost	Total Market	Total Lower of C or M
A90	~~35~~ 25	$59	$ 57	$1,475	$1,425	
	10	58		580	570	
				2,055	1,995	$1,995
C18	16		200			
D41	24		140			
E34	125		26			
F17	18		550			
G68	60		15			
K41	5		390			
Q79	375		6			
R72	100		17			
S60	6		235			
W21	140		18			
Z35	9		700			

Page not used.

PROBLEM 8-5 ___

1. *Omit "00" in the cents columns.*

	COST	RETAIL

PROBLEM 8-5 ___, Concluded

2. a. *Omit "00" in the cents columns.*

b. *Omit "00" in the cents columns.*

EXERCISE 9-1

a. New printing press costs debited to the asset account:

b. Secondhand printing press costs debited to the asset account:

EXERCISE 9-2

a.

b.

EXERCISE 9-3

EXERCISE 9-4

a. ____

____

____

____

b. ____

____

____

____

EXERCISE 9-5

a. 20 years: ____________________

b. 25 years: ____________________

c. 40 years: ____________________

d. 4 years: ____________________

e. 5 years: ____________________

f. 10 years: ____________________

g. 50 years: ____________________

EXERCISE 9-6

____

____

EXERCISE 9-7

____

____

____

____

EXERCISE 9-8

a.

Truck No.	Cost	Estimated Residual Value	Estimated Useful Life (miles)	Accumulated Depreciation at Beginning of Year	Miles Operated During Year	Depr. Rate per Mile	Credit to Accumulated Depreciation
1	$68,000	$8,000	300,000	$27,000	40,000	$______	$__________
2	48,600	6,600	200,000	39,900	12,000	$______	$__________
3	38,000	3,000	200,000	8,050	36,000	$______	$__________
4	28,000	4,000	120,000	—	21,000	$______	$__________
Total							$__________

Name ______________________________________

EXERCISE 9-8, Concluded

b.

JOURNAL PAGE

	DATE		DESCRIPTION	POST. REF.	DEBIT	CREDIT	
1							1
2							2
3							3

EXERCISE 9-9

a. Straight-line method:

First year: ______________________________

Second year: ______________________________

b. Declining-balance method, at twice the straight-line rate:

First year: ______________________________

Second year: ______________________________

EXERCISE 9-10

a. Straight-line method:

____

b. Declining-balance method, at twice the straight-line rate:

First year: ______________________________

Second year: ______________________________

EXERCISE 9-11

a. Straight-line method:

First year: ______________________________

Second year: ______________________________

b. Declining-balance method, at twice the straight-line rate:

First year: ______________________________

Second year: ______________________________

EXERCISE 9-12

a. ______________________________

b. ______________________________

c. ______________________________

EXERCISE 9-13

a.

	CURRENT YEAR	PRECEDING YEAR

Explanation of differences:

b.

EXERCISE 9-14

1.
2.
3.
4.
5.
6.
7.
8.
9.
10.

EXERCISE 9-15

1. ______________________________
2. ______________________________
3. ______________________________
4. ______________________________
5. ______________________________
6. ______________________________
7. ______________________________
8. ______________________________
9. ______________________________
10. ______________________________

EXERCISE 9-16

a. – c.

JOURNAL PAGE

	DATE		DESCRIPTION	POST. REF.	DEBIT	CREDIT	
1							1
2							2
3							3
4							4
5							5
6							6
7							7
8							8
9							9
10							10
11							11
12							12
13							13
14							14
15							15
16							16
17							17

EXERCISE 9-17

a. ______

b. ______

EXERCISE 9-18

a. ______

b. (1) and (2)

JOURNAL PAGE

	DATE		DESCRIPTION	POST. REF.	DEBIT	CREDIT	
1							1
2							2
3							3
4							4
5							5
6							6
7							7

Name ______________________________

EXERCISE 9-25

EXERCISE 9-26

a.

b.

JOURNAL

PAGE

	DATE		DESCRIPTION	POST. REF.	DEBIT	CREDIT	
1							1
2							2
3							3
4							4

EXERCISE 9-27

a.

b.

JOURNAL

PAGE

	DATE		DESCRIPTION	POST. REF.	DEBIT	CREDIT	
1							1
2							2
3							3
4							4

EXERCISE 9-28

EXERCISE 9-29

a. Current year:

Preceding year:

b.

EXERCISE 9-30

a. 2002: ______________________________

____

2001: ______________________________

____

b.

____

____

____

____

____

____

____

____

____

____

____

____

____

APPENDIX EXERCISE 9-31

First year: ______________________________

____

Second year: ______________________________

____

APPENDIX EXERCISE 9-32

First year: ______________________________

____

Second year: ______________________________

____

APPENDIX EXERCISE 9-33

First year: ______________________________

____

Second year: ______________________________

____

Page not used.

Name ______________________________

PROBLEM 9-2 ___

	Depreciation Expense		
Year	**a. Straight-Line Method**	**b. Units-of-Production Method**	**c. Declining-Balance Method**
______	______	______	______
______	______	______	______
______	______	______	______
______	______	______	______
Total	______	______	______

Calculations:

PROBLEM 9-2 ___, Concluded

PROBLEM 9-3 ___

a.

STRAIGHT-LINE METHOD

Year	Calculations	Depreciation Expense
2005		
2006		
2007		
2008		

b.

UNITS-OF-PRODUCTION METHOD

Year	Calculations	Depreciation Expense
2005		
2006		
2007		
2008		

PROBLEM 9-3 ___, Concluded

c.

DECLINING-BALANCE METHOD

Year	Calculations	Depreciation Expense
2005		
2006		
2007		
2008		

PROBLEM 9-5 ___

JOURNAL

PAGE

	DATE		DESCRIPTION	POST. REF.	DEBIT	CREDIT	
1							1
2							2
3							3
4							4
5							5
6							6
7							7
8							8
9							9
10							10
11							11
12							12
13							13
14							14
15							15
16							16
17							17
18							18
19							19
20							20
21							21
22							22
23							23
24							24
25							25
26							26
27							27
28							28
29							29
30							30
31							31
32							32
33							33
34							34
35							35
36							36

PROBLEM 9-5 ___, Concluded

JOURNAL

PAGE

DATE	DESCRIPTION	POST. REF.	DEBIT	CREDIT

PROBLEM 9-6 ___

1.

2.

JOURNAL

PAGE

	DATE		DESCRIPTION	POST. REF.	DEBIT	CREDIT	
1							1
2							2
3							3
4							4
5							5
6							6
7							7
8							8
9							9
10							10
11							11
12							12

Page not used.

EXERCISE 10-1

EXERCISE 10-2

a. 1. through b. 2.

JOURNAL PAGE

	DATE		DESCRIPTION	POST. REF.	DEBIT	CREDIT	
1							1
2							2
3							3
4							4
5							5
6							6
7							7
8							8
9							9
10							10
11							11
12							12
13							13
14							14
15							15
16							16
17							17
18							18
19							19
20							20

EXERCISE 10-3

a. (1) ____________________

(2) ____________________

b. (1) ____________________

(2) ____________________

c. ____________________

EXERCISE 10-4

a. and b.

JOURNAL PAGE

	DATE		DESCRIPTION	POST. REF.	DEBIT	CREDIT	
1							1
2							2
3							3
4							4
5							5
6							6
7							7
8							8
9							9
10							10
11							11
12							12

EXERCISE 10-5

a.–c.

JOURNAL PAGE

	DATE		DESCRIPTION	POST. REF.	DEBIT	CREDIT	
1							1
2							2
3							3
4							4
5							5
6							6
7							7
8							8
9							9
10							10
11							11
12							12

EXERCISE 10-6

a. ______________________

b. ______________________

c. ______________________

EXERCISE 10-7

a. and b.

JOURNAL PAGE

	DATE		DESCRIPTION	POST. REF.	DEBIT	CREDIT	
1							1
2							2
3							3
4							4
5							5
6							6

EXERCISE 10-8

a.

b.

JOURNAL PAGE

	DATE		DESCRIPTION	POST. REF.	DEBIT	CREDIT	
1							1
2							2
3							3
4							4

c.

EXERCISE 10-9

a.

JOURNAL PAGE

	DATE		DESCRIPTION	POST. REF.	DEBIT	CREDIT	
1							1
2							2
3							3
4							4

b.

EXERCISE 10-10

a. and b.

JOURNAL PAGE

	DATE		DESCRIPTION	POST. REF.	DEBIT	CREDIT	
1							1
2							2
3							3
4							4
5							5
6							6

c.

EXERCISE 10-11

a.

b.

EXERCISE 10-12

	Consultant	**Computer Programmer**	**Administrator**
Regular earnings	$	$	$
Overtime earnings			
Gross pay	$	$	$
Less: Social security tax	$	$	$
Medicare tax			
Federal income tax withheld			
	$	$	$
Net pay	$	$	$

EXERCISE 10-13

a. Earnings:

1. At regular rate	$ ______
2. At overtime rate	44,200
3. Total earnings	______
Deductions:	
4. Social security tax	15,730
5. Medicare tax	4,035
6. Income tax withheld	47,915
7. Medical insurance	7,860
8. Union dues	______
9. Total deductions	80,000
10. Net amount paid	189,000
Accounts debited:	
11. Factory Wages	135,400
12. Sales Salaries	______
13. Office Salaries	57,800

b. and c.

JOURNAL PAGE

	DATE		DESCRIPTION	POST. REF.	DEBIT	CREDIT	
1							1
2							2
3							3
4							4
5							5
6							6
7							7
8							8
9							9
10							10
11							11
12							12

d. ____

EXERCISE 10-14

EXERCISE 10-15

a.

b.

c.

d.

e.

EXERCISE 10-16

a.

b.

JOURNAL PAGE

	DATE		DESCRIPTION	POST. REF.	DEBIT	CREDIT	
1							1
2							2
3							3
4							4
5							5
6							6
7							7
8							8
9							9

EXERCISE 10-17

EXERCISE 10-18

JOURNAL PAGE

	DATE		DESCRIPTION	POST. REF.	DEBIT	CREDIT	
1							1
2							2
3							3

EXERCISE 10-19

a. and b.

JOURNAL PAGE

	DATE		DESCRIPTION	POST. REF.	DEBIT	CREDIT	
1							1
2							2
3							3
4							4
5							5
6							6

EXERCISE 10-20

EXERCISE 10-21

a. 2006: ______________________

2005: ______________________

b. ______________________

EXERCISE 10-22

a. Apple Computer Inc: ______________________

Dell Computer Corp.: ______________________

b. ______________________

Page not used.

PROBLEM 10-1 ___

1. and 2.

JOURNAL

PAGE

	DATE		DESCRIPTION	POST. REF.	DEBIT	CREDIT	
1							1
2							2
3							3
4							4
5							5
6							6
7							7
8							8
9							9
10							10
11							11
12							12
13							13
14							14
15							15
16							16
17							17
18							18
19							19
20							20
21							21
22							22
23							23
24							24
25							25
26							26
27							27
28							28
29							29
30							30
31							31
32							32
33							33
34							34
35							35
36							36

PROBLEM 10-1 ___, Concluded

JOURNAL

PAGE

DATE		DESCRIPTION	POST. REF.	DEBIT	CREDIT

Name ______________________________

PROBLEM 10-3 ___

1.

Employee	Gross Earnings	Federal Income Tax Withheld	Social Security Tax Withheld	Medicare Tax Withheld

2. Payroll taxes incurred and paid by employer:

a. Social security tax paid by employer............................ $ ____________

b. Medicare tax paid by employer.................................... ____________

c. State unemployment compensation tax....................... ____________

d. Federal unemployment compensation tax.................. ____________

e. Total payroll taxes expense.. $ ____________

Page not used.

PROBLEM 10-4 ___

PAYROLL FOR THE WEEK ENDED *December 12, 2006*

		EARNINGS			DEDUCTIONS					PAID		ACCOUNTS DEBITED		
NAME	TOTAL HOURS	REGULAR	OVER-TIME	TOTAL	SOCIAL SECU-RITY TAX	MEDI-CARE TAX	FEDERAL INCOME TAX	MEDICAL INSUR-ANCE	TOTAL	NET AMOUNT	CK. NO.	SALES SALARIES EXPENSE	OFFICE SALARIES EXPENSE	DELIVERY SALARIES EXPENSE
Alvarez, Julio	43.00	600.00	67.50	667.50	40.05	10.01	106.80	28.20	185.06	482.44	632	667.50		
Christy, T. Howard	45.00	480.00	90.00	570.00	34.20	8.55	85.50	46.70	174.95	395.05	633	570.00		
Davis, Lyn	40.00	720.00		720.00	43.20	10.80	104.40	26.30	184.70	535.30	634			720.00
Gunwald, Jenny		1,500.00		1,500.00	90.00	22.50	285.00	85.00	482.50	1,017.50	635		1,500.00	
Jenkins, Sara	46.00	840.00	189.00	1,029.00	61.74	15.44	180.08	75.00	332.25	696.75	636	1,029.00		
Ouchi, T.		1,400.00		1,400.00	84.00	21.00	252.0	95.00	452.00	948.00	637		1,400.00	
Peters, Ken	50.00	800.00	300.00	1,100.00	66.00	16.50	192.50	70.40	345.40	754.60	638	1,100.00		
Raines, Frank	47.00	720.00	189.00	909.00	54.54	13.64	154.53	24.50	247.21	661.80	639			909.00
Wilson, T. J.	38.00	330.00		330.00	19.80	4.95	41.25	18.10	84.10	245.90	640			330.00
		7,390.00	835.50	8,225.50	493.53	123.38	1,402.06	469.20	2,488.17	5,737.33		3,366.50	2,900.00	1,959.00

PROBLEM 10-4 ___, Concluded

1.–4.

JOURNAL

PAGE

DATE		DESCRIPTION	POST. REF.	DEBIT	CREDIT

Name ____

PROBLEM 10-5 ___

1. *The payroll register form is on pages 374 and 375.*

2.

JOURNAL PAGE

	DATE		DESCRIPTION	POST. REF.	DEBIT	CREDIT	
1							1
2							2
3							3
4							4
5							5
6							6
7							7
8							8
9							9
10							10
11							11
12							12
13							13
14							14
15							15
16							16
17							17
18							18
19							19
20							20
21							21
22							22
23							23
24							24
25							25
26							26
27							27
28							28
29							29
30							30
31							31
32							32
33							33
34							34
35							35

PROBLEM 10-5 ___, Continued

1.

PAYROLL FOR WEEK ENDING

NAME	TOTAL HOURS	EARNINGS			DEDUCTIONS	
		REGULAR	OVERTIME	TOTAL	SOCIAL SECURITY TAX	MEDICARE TAX

Name ______________________________

PROBLEM 10-5 ___, Concluded

December 7, 2006

			PAID		ACCOUNTS DEBITED	
FEDERAL INCOME TAX	U.S. SAVINGS BONDS	TOTAL	NET AMOUNT	CK. NO.	SALES SALARIES EXPENSE	OFFICE SALARIES EXPENSE

Page not used.

PROBLEM 10-6 ___

1. and 2.

JOURNAL

PAGE

DATE		DESCRIPTION	POST. REF.	DEBIT	CREDIT

PROBLEM 10-6 ___, Continued

JOURNAL

PAGE

	DATE		DESCRIPTION	POST. REF.	DEBIT	CREDIT	
1							1
2							2
3							3
4							4
5							5
6							6
7							7
8							8
9							9
10							10
11							11
12							12
13							13
14							14
15							15
16							16
17							17
18							18
19							19
20							20
21							21
22							22
23							23
24							24
25							25
26							26
27							27
28							28
29							29
30							30
31							31
32							32
33							33
34							34
35							35
36							36

PROBLEM 10-6 ___, Continued

JOURNAL

PAGE

	DATE		DESCRIPTION	POST. REF.	DEBIT	CREDIT	
1							1
2							2
3							3
4							4
5							5
6							6
7							7
8							8
9							9
10							10
11							11
12							12
13							13
14							14
15							15
16							16
17							17
18							18
19							19
20							20
21							21
22							22
23							23
24							24
25							25
26							26
27							27
28							28
29							29
30							30
31							31
32							32
33							33
34							34
35							35
36							36

PROBLEM 10-6 ___, Concluded

JOURNAL

PAGE

	DATE	DESCRIPTION	POST. REF.	DEBIT	CREDIT	
1						1
2						2
3						3
4						4
5						5
6						6
7						7
8						8
9						9
10						10
11						11
12						12
13						13
14						14
15						15
16						16
17						17
18						18
19						19
20						20
21						21
22						22
23						23
24						24
25						25
26						26
27						27
28						28
29						29
30						30
31						31
32						32
33						33
34						34
35						35
36						36

COMPREHENSIVE PROBLEM 3

1.

JOURNAL

PAGE

DATE		DESCRIPTION	POST. REF.	DEBIT	CREDIT

COMPREHENSIVE PROBLEM 3, Continued

JOURNAL

PAGE

DATE		DESCRIPTION	POST. REF.	DEBIT	CREDIT

COMPREHENSIVE PROBLEM 3, Continued

2.

COMPREHENSIVE PROBLEM 3, Continued

3. and 4.

JOURNAL

PAGE

DATE	DESCRIPTION	POST. REF.	DEBIT	CREDIT

COMPREHENSIVE PROBLEM 3, Continued

JOURNAL

PAGE

	DATE		DESCRIPTION	POST. REF.	DEBIT	CREDIT	
1							1
2							2
3							3
4							4
5							5
6							6
7							7
8							8
9							9
10							10
11							11
12							12
13							13
14							14
15							15
16							16
17							17
18							18
19							19
20							20
21							21
22							22
23							23
24							24
25							25
26							26
27							27
28							28
29							29
30							30
31							31
32							32
33							33
34							34
35							35
36							36

COMPREHENSIVE PROBLEM 3, Continued

5. *Omit "00" in the cents columns.*

COMPREHENSIVE PROBLEM 3, Continued

COMPREHENSIVE PROBLEM 3, Concluded

6.

EXERCISE 11-1

Description	1st Year	2nd Year	3rd Year	4th Year	5th Year
Total Preferred Stock					
Total Common Stock					
Dividend Totals	$0	$40,000	$80,000	$120,000	$140,000
Per Share—Preferred					
Per Share—Common					

EXERCISE 11-2

Description	1st Year	2nd Year	3rd Year	4th Year	5th Year
Total Preferred Stock					
Total Common Stock					
Dividend Totals	$0	$45,000	$110,000	$130,000	$180,000
Per Share—Preferred					
Per Share—Common					

EXERCISE 11-3

a.

JOURNAL PAGE

	DATE		DESCRIPTION	POST. REF.	DEBIT	CREDIT	
1							1
2							2
3							3
4							4
5							5
6							6
7							7
8							8
9							9
10							10
11							11

b. ____________________

EXERCISE 11-4

a.

JOURNAL PAGE

	DATE	DESCRIPTION	POST. REF.	DEBIT	CREDIT	
1						1
2						2
3						3
4						4
5						5
6						6
7						7
8						8
9						9

b.

EXERCISE 11-5

JOURNAL PAGE

	DATE	DESCRIPTION	POST. REF.	DEBIT	CREDIT	
1						1
2						2
3						3

EXERCISE 11-6

a.–c.

JOURNAL PAGE

	DATE	DESCRIPTION	POST. REF.	DEBIT	CREDIT	
1						1
2						2
3						3
4						4
5						5
6						6
7						7
8						8
9						9
10						10
11						11
12						12
13						13
14						14

EXERCISE 11-7

JOURNAL PAGE

	DATE		DESCRIPTION	POST. REF.	DEBIT	CREDIT	
1							1
2							2
3							3
4							4
5							5
6							6
7							7
8							8
9							9
10							10
11							11
12							12

EXERCISE 11-8

JOURNAL PAGE

	DATE		DESCRIPTION	POST. REF.	DEBIT	CREDIT	
1							1
2							2
3							3
4							4
5							5
6							6
7							7
8							8
9							9
10							10
11							11
12							12
13							13
14							14
15							15
16							16
17							17
18							18

EXERCISE 11-9

a.

JOURNAL PAGE

	DATE		DESCRIPTION	POST. REF.	DEBIT	CREDIT	
1							1
2							2
3							3
4							4
5							5
6							6
7							7
8							8
9							9
10							10
11							11
12							12

b.

c. ______________________________

____

____

____

EXERCISE 11-10

a.

JOURNAL PAGE

	DATE		DESCRIPTION	POST. REF.	DEBIT	CREDIT	
1							1
2							2
3							3
4							4
5							5
6							6
7							7
8							8
9							9
10							10
11							11
12							12
13							13

EXERCISE 11-10, Concluded

b.

c. ______________________

d. ______________________

EXERCISE 11-11

a.

JOURNAL PAGE

	DATE		DESCRIPTION	POST. REF.	DEBIT	CREDIT	
1							1
2							2
3							3
4							4
5							5
6							6
7							7
8							8
9							9
10							10
11							11
12							12
13							13

b. ______________________

c. ______________________

d. ______________________

EXERCISE 11-12

a. ______________________________

b. ______________________________

EXERCISE 11-13

	Assets	Liabilities	Stockholders' Equity
(1) Declaring a cash dividend	______	______	______
(2) Paying the cash dividend declared in (1)	______	______	______
(3) Authorizing and issuing stock certificates in a stock split	______	______	______
(4) Declaring a stock dividend	______	______	______
(5) Issuing stock certificates for the stock dividend declared in (4)	______	______	______

EXERCISE 11-14

JOURNAL PAGE

	DATE		DESCRIPTION	POST. REF.	DEBIT	CREDIT	
1							1
2							2
3							3
4							4
5							5
6							6
7							7

EXERCISE 11-15

a. (1) and (2)

JOURNAL PAGE

	DATE		DESCRIPTION	POST. REF.	DEBIT	CREDIT	
1							1
2							2
3							3
4							4
5							5
6							6
7							7
9							9

EXERCISE 11-15, Concluded

b. **(1)** Total paid-in capital: ____________________

(2) Total retained earnings: ____________________

(3) Total stockholders' equity: ____________________

c. **(1)** Total paid-in capital: ____________________

(2) Total retained earnings: ____________________

(3) Total stockholders' equity: ____________________

EXERCISE 11-16

JOURNAL PAGE

DATE	DESCRIPTION	POST. REF.	DEBIT	CREDIT

EXERCISE 11-17

EXERCISE 11-18

EXERCISE 11-19

EXERCISE 11-20

	COMMON STOCK, $2 PAR	PAID-IN CAPITAL IN EXCESS OF PAR	TREASURY STOCK	RETAINED EARNINGS	TOTAL

Name ____________________

EXERCISE 11-21

EXERCISE 11-22

EXERCISE 11-23

EXERCISE 11-24

a.

b.

Name ____

PROBLEM 11-1 ___

1.

Year	**Total Dividends**	**Preferred Dividends**		**Common Dividends**	
		Total	**Per Share**	**Total**	**Per Share**
2002					
2003					
2004					
2005					
2006					
2007					

Supporting calculations:

PROBLEM 11-1 ___, Concluded

2.

3.

Name ________________________________

PROBLEM 11-2 ___

JOURNAL

PAGE

	DATE	DESCRIPTION	POST. REF.	DEBIT	CREDIT	
1						1
2						2
3						3
4						4
5						5
6						6
7						7
8						8
9						9
10						10
11						11
12						12
13						13
14						14
15						15
16						16
17						17
18						18
19						19
20						20
21						21
22						22
23						23
24						24
25						25
26						26
27						27
28						28
29						29
30						30
31						31
32						32
33						33
34						34
35						35
36						36

PROBLEM 11-2 ___, Concluded

JOURNAL

PAGE

DATE		DESCRIPTION	POST. REF.	DEBIT	CREDIT

PROBLEM 11-3 ___

a.–g.

JOURNAL

PAGE

DATE	DESCRIPTION	POST. REF.	DEBIT	CREDIT

PROBLEM 11-3 ___, Concluded

JOURNAL

PAGE

DATE		DESCRIPTION	POST. REF.	DEBIT	CREDIT

PROBLEM 11-4 ___

1. and 2.

Common Stock

Paid-In Capital in Excess of Stated Value

Retained Earnings

Treasury Stock

Paid-In Capital from Sale of Treasury Stock

PROBLEM 11-4 ___, Continued

Stock Dividends Distributable

Stock Dividends

Cash Dividends

PROBLEM 11-4 ___, Continued

2.

JOURNAL PAGE

DATE		DESCRIPTION	POST. REF.	DEBIT	CREDIT

PROBLEM 11-4 ___, Concluded

3.

4.

Name ______________________________

PROBLEM 11-5 ___

JOURNAL PAGE

	DATE		DESCRIPTION	POST. REF.	DEBIT	CREDIT	
1							1
2							2
3							3
4							4
5							5
6							6
7							7
8							8
9							9
10							10
11							11
12							12
13							13
14							14
15							15
16							16
17							17
18							18
19							19
20							20
21							21
22							22
23							23
24							24
25							25
26							26
27							27
28							28
29							29
30							30
31							31
32							32
33							33
34							34
35							35
36							36

PROBLEM 11-5 ___, Concluded

JOURNAL

PAGE

DATE		DESCRIPTION	POST. REF.	DEBIT	CREDIT

EXERCISE 12-1

JOURNAL PAGE

	DATE		DESCRIPTION	POST. REF.	DEBIT	CREDIT	
1							1
2							2
3							3
4							4
5							5
6							6
7							7
8							8
9							9
10							10
11							11
12							12
13							13
14							14
15							15

EXERCISE 12-2

JOURNAL PAGE

	DATE		DESCRIPTION	POST. REF.	DEBIT	CREDIT	
1							1
2							2
3							3
4							4
5							5
6							6
7							7
8							8
9							9
10							10
11							11
12							12
13							13
14							14
15							15

EXERCISE 12-3

a.

b.

JOURNAL

PAGE

	DATE		DESCRIPTION	POST. REF.	DEBIT	CREDIT	
1							1
2							2
3							3
4							4
5							5

c.

EXERCISE 12-4

a.

JOURNAL PAGE

	DATE		DESCRIPTION	POST. REF.	DEBIT	CREDIT	
1							1
2							2
3							3
4							4
5							5
6							6

b.

EXERCISE 12-5

a. and b.

JOURNAL PAGE

	DATE		DESCRIPTION	POST. REF.	DEBIT	CREDIT	
1							1
2							2
3							3
4							4
5							5
6							6
7							7
8							8

EXERCISE 12-5, Concluded

c. Balance sheet disclosure:

Note disclosure:

EXERCISE 12-6

a.

EXERCISE 12-6, Concluded

b. and c.

JOURNAL

PAGE

	DATE		DESCRIPTION	POST. REF.	DEBIT	CREDIT	
1							1
2							2
3							3
4							4
5							5
6							6

d. Balance sheet disclosure:

e. Note disclosure:

EXERCISE 12-7

a. and c.

JOURNAL PAGE

	DATE		DESCRIPTION	POST. REF.	DEBIT	CREDIT	
1							1
2							2
3							3
4							4
5							5
6							6
7							7
8							8
9							9

b. Balance sheet disclosure:

Note disclosure:

EXERCISE 12-8

a. and b.

JOURNAL PAGE

	DATE		DESCRIPTION	POST. REF.	DEBIT	CREDIT	
1							1
2							2
3							3
4							4
5							5
6							6

c. Balance sheet disclosure:

EXERCISE 12-9

EXERCISE 12-10

EXERCISE 12-11

a. ______________________ e. ______________________

b. ______________________ f. ______________________

c. ______________________ g. ______________________

d. ______________________ h. ______________________

EXERCISE 12-12

EXERCISE 12-13

EXERCISE 12-14

EXERCISE 12-15

a. – c.

EXERCISE 12-16

a.

b.

c.

d.

e.

f.

g.

h.

Name ______________________________

EXERCISE 12-17

a.

b.

EXERCISE 12-18

a.– c.

EXERCISE 12-19

a. and b.

JOURNAL PAGE

	DATE		DESCRIPTION	POST. REF.	DEBIT	CREDIT	
1							1
2							2
3							3
4							4
5							5
6							6
7							7
8							8

EXERCISE 12-20

a.

Name ______________________________

EXERCISE 12-20, Concluded

b.

EXERCISE 12-21

a.–c.

JOURNAL PAGE

	DATE		DESCRIPTION	POST. REF.	DEBIT	CREDIT	
1							1
2							2
3							3
4							4
5							5
6							6
7							7
8							8
9							9
10							10
11							11
12							12
13							13

EXERCISE 12-22

a. and b.

JOURNAL PAGE

	DATE		DESCRIPTION	POST. REF.	DEBIT	CREDIT	
1							1
2							2
3							3
4							4
5							5
6							6
7							7

EXERCISE 12-23

a. and b.

EXERCISE 12-24

a. (1) and (2)

b.

EXERCISE 12-25

a. and b.

EXERCISE 12-25, Concluded

c.

EXERCISE 12-26

a.

b.

PROBLEM 12-1 ___

1. and 2.

Year	Income Tax Deducted on Income Statement	Income Tax Payments for the Year	Deferred Income Tax Payable	
			Year's Addition (Deduction)	Year-End Balance
First				
Second				
Third				
Fourth				
Total				

Page not used.

PROBLEM 12-2 ___

Omit "00" in the cents columns.

PROBLEM 12-2 ___, Concluded

PROBLEM 12-3 ___

1.

PROBLEM 12-3 ___, Continued

2.

PROBLEM 12-3 ___, Continued

3.

PROBLEM 12-3 ___, Concluded

PROBLEM 12-4 ___

JOURNAL

PAGE

DATE		DESCRIPTION	POST. REF.	DEBIT	CREDIT

PROBLEM 12-4 ___, Concluded

JOURNAL

PAGE

DATE		DESCRIPTION	POST. REF.	DEBIT	CREDIT

EXERCISE 13-1

	(a)	(b)	(c)
Earnings before bond interest and income tax	$1,600,000	$2,400,000	$4,000,000
Bond interest			
Balance			
Income tax			
Net income			
Dividends on preferred stock			
Earnings available for common stock			
Earnings per share on common stock			

EXERCISE 13-2

EXERCISE 13-3

EXERCISE 13-4

a.

b.

EXERCISE 13-5

a.

b.

EXERCISE 13-6

EXERCISE 13-7

Name ________________________________

EXERCISE 13-8

EXERCISE 13-9

EXERCISE 13-10

EXERCISE 13-11

JOURNAL

PAGE

	DATE		DESCRIPTION	POST. REF.	DEBIT	CREDIT	
1							1
2							2
3							3
4							4
5							5
6							6
7							7
8							8
9							9
10							10

EXERCISE 13-12

a. 1.–4.

JOURNAL

PAGE

	DATE		DESCRIPTION	POST. REF.	DEBIT	CREDIT	
1							1
2							2
3							3
4							4
5							5
6							6
7							7
8							8
9							9
10							10
11							11
12							12
13							13
14							14
15							15

b. ____

____

____

____

EXERCISE 13-12, Concluded

Supporting calculations:

EXERCISE 13-13

a. and b.

JOURNAL PAGE

	DATE		DESCRIPTION	POST. REF.	DEBIT	CREDIT	
1							1
2							2
3							3
4							4
5							5
6							6
7							7

Supporting calculations:

EXERCISE 13-14

JOURNAL

PAGE

DATE		DESCRIPTION	POST. REF.	DEBIT	CREDIT

EXERCISE 13-15

JOURNAL

PAGE

DATE		DESCRIPTION	POST. REF.	DEBIT	CREDIT

EXERCISE 13-16

EXERCISE 13-17

EXERCISE 13-18

a.–d.

JOURNAL PAGE

	DATE		DESCRIPTION	POST. REF.	DEBIT	CREDIT	
1							1
2							2
3							3
4							4
5							5
6							6
7							7
8							8
9							9
10							10
11							11
12							12
13							13
14							14
15							15

EXERCISE 13-19

a.–d.

JOURNAL PAGE

	DATE		DESCRIPTION	POST. REF.	DEBIT	CREDIT	
1							1
2							2
3							3
4							4
5							5
6							6
7							7
8							8
9							9
10							10
11							11
12							12
13							13
14							14
15							15
16							16
17							17

EXERCISE 13-20

a. Current year: ______________________________

____

____

Preceding year: ______________________________

____

____

b. ______________________________

____

____

____

____

____

____

____

____

APPENDIX EXERCISE 13-21

a. 1.–4.

JOURNAL PAGE

	DATE		DESCRIPTION	POST. REF.	DEBIT	CREDIT	
1							1
2							2
3							3
4							4
5							5
6							6
7							7
8							8
9							9
10							10
11							11
12							12
13							13

Supporting calculations:

b.

APPENDIX EXERCISE 13-22

a. 1.–3.

JOURNAL PAGE

	DATE		DESCRIPTION	POST. REF.	DEBIT	CREDIT	
1							1
2							2
3							3
4							4
5							5
6							6
7							7
8							8
9							9
10							10
11							11
12							12
13							13
14							14
15							15

Supporting calculations:

b.

Name ____

APPENDIX EXERCISE 13-23

a.–d.

APPENDIX EXERCISE 13-24

a.–d.

PROBLEM 13-1 ___

1.

	Plan 1	Plan 2	Plan 3
Earnings before interest and income tax			
Deduct interest on bonds			
Income before income tax			
Deduct income tax			
Net income			
Dividends on preferred stock			
Available for dividends on common stock			
Shares of common stock outstanding			
Earnings per share on common stock			

2.

	Plan 1	Plan 2	Plan 3
Earnings before interest and income tax			
Deduct interest on bonds			
Income before income tax			
Deduct income tax			
Net income			
Dividends on preferred stock			
Available for dividends on common stock			
Shares of common stock outstanding			
Earnings per share on common stock			

PROBLEM 13-1 ___, Concluded

3.

Name ______________________________________

PROBLEM 13-2 ___

1. and 2.

JOURNAL

PAGE

DATE	DESCRIPTION	POST. REF.	DEBIT	CREDIT

PROBLEM 13-2 ___, Concluded

JOURNAL

PAGE

	DATE		DESCRIPTION	POST. REF.	DEBIT	CREDIT	
1							1
2							2
3							3
4							4
5							5
6							6
7							7
8							8
9							9
10							10
11							11
12							12
13							13
14							14
15							15
16							16
17							17
18							18
19							19

3.

4.

Name ______________________

PROBLEM 13-3 ___

1. and 2.

JOURNAL

PAGE

DATE		DESCRIPTION	POST. REF.	DEBIT	CREDIT

PROBLEM 13-3 ___, Concluded

JOURNAL

PAGE

DATE		DESCRIPTION	POST. REF.	DEBIT	CREDIT

3.

4.

Name ____

PROBLEM 13-4 ___

1.

JOURNAL

PAGE

DATE		DESCRIPTION	POST. REF.	DEBIT	CREDIT

PROBLEM 13-4 ___, Concluded

JOURNAL PAGE

	DATE		DESCRIPTION	POST. REF.	DEBIT	CREDIT	
1							1
2							2
3							3
4							4
5							5
6							6
7							7
8							8
9							9
10							10
11							11
12							12
13							13
14							14
15							15
16							16
17							17
18							18
19							19

2. (a) 2005: ______________________________

(b) 2006: ______________________________

3.

Name ____

PROBLEM 13-5 ___

JOURNAL

PAGE

	DATE	DESCRIPTION	POST. REF.	DEBIT	CREDIT	
1						1
2						2
3						3
4						4
5						5
6						6
7						7
8						8
9						9
10						10
11						11
12						12
13						13
14						14
15						15
16						16
17						17
18						18
19						19
20						20
21						21
22						22
23						23
24						24
25						25
26						26
27						27
28						28
29						29
30						30
31						31
32						32
33						33
34						34
35						35
36						36

PROBLEM 13-5 ___, Concluded

JOURNAL

PAGE

DATE		DESCRIPTION	POST. REF.	DEBIT	CREDIT

APPENDIX PROBLEM 13-6 ___

1. a. and b.

JOURNAL PAGE

	DATE		DESCRIPTION	POST. REF.	DEBIT	CREDIT	
1							1
2							2
3							3
4							4
5							5
6							6
7							7
8							8
9							9
10							10
11							11
12							12
13							13
14							14
15							15
16							16
17							17
18							18
19							19

2.

APPENDIX PROBLEM 13-7 ___

1. a. and b.

JOURNAL PAGE

	DATE		DESCRIPTION	POST. REF.	DEBIT	CREDIT	
1							1
2							2
3							3
4							4
5							5
6							6
7							7
8							8
9							9
10							10
11							11
12							12
13							13
14							14
15							15
16							16
17							17
18							18
19							19

2.

Name ________________________________

COMPREHENSIVE PROBLEM 4

1.

JOURNAL

PAGE

DATE	DESCRIPTION	POST. REF.	DEBIT	CREDIT

COMPREHENSIVE PROBLEM 4, Continued

JOURNAL

PAGE

DATE		DESCRIPTION	POST. REF.	DEBIT	CREDIT

COMPREHENSIVE PROBLEM 4, Continued

2. a. *Omit "00" in the cents columns.*

Income Statement

COMPREHENSIVE PROBLEM 4, Continued

Income Statement (Concluded)

COMPREHENSIVE PROBLEM 4, Continued

2. b. *Omit "00" in the cents columns.*

Retained Earnings Statement

COMPREHENSIVE PROBLEM 4, Continued

2. c. *Omit "00" in the cents columns.*

Balance Sheet

COMPREHENSIVE PROBLEM 4, Concluded

Balance Sheet (Concluded)

Page not used.

EXERCISE 14-1

EXERCISE 14-2

a. ______________________________

b. ______________________________

c. ______________________________

d. ______________________________

e. ______________________________

f. ______________________________

g. ______________________________

h. ______________________________

EXERCISE 14-3

a. Purchased patents: ______________________________

b. Purchased buildings: ______________________________

c. Purchased treasury stock: ______________________________

d. Sold equipment: ______________________________

e. Net income: ______________________________

f. Issued preferred stock: ______________________________

g. Redeemed bonds: ______________________________

h. Paid cash dividends: ______________________________

i. Sold long-term investments: ______________________________

j. Issued common stock: ______________________________

k. Issued bonds: ______________________________

EXERCISE 14-4

a. Increase in notes payable due in 90 days to vendors: ____________________

b. Loss on disposal of fixed assets: ____________________

c. Decrease in accounts payable: ____________________

d. Increase in notes receivable due in 90 days from customers: ____________________

e. Decrease in salaries payable: ____________________

f. Decrease in prepaid expenses: ____________________

g. Depreciation of fixed assets: ____________________

h. Decrease in accounts receivable: ____________________

i. Amortization of patent: ____________________

j. Increase in merchandise inventory: ____________________

k. Gain on retirement of long-term debt: ____________________

EXERCISE 14-5

a.

b. ____________________

EXERCISE 14-6

EXERCISE 14-7

EXERCISE 14-8

EXERCISE 14-9

EXERCISE 14-10

EXERCISE 14-11

EXERCISE 14-12

EXERCISE 14-13

EXERCISE 14-14

EXERCISE 14-15

EXERCISE 14-16

a.

b.

EXERCISE 14-17

EXERCISE 14-18

a.

b.

EXERCISE 14-19

EXERCISE 14-20

EXERCISE 14-21

Name ____

EXERCISE 14-22

EXERCISE 14-23

EXERCISE 14-24

a. and b.

	Fiscal Years Ended	
	2003	2002

c.

PROBLEM 14-1 ___

Omit "00" in the cents columns.

PROBLEM 14-1 ___, Continued

PROBLEM 14-1 ___, Continued

The use of this form is not required unless so indicated by the instructor.

Work Sheet for Statement of Cash Flows

ACCOUNTS	BALANCE, ________, 2005	TRANSACTIONS		BALANCE, ________, 2006
		DEBIT	CREDIT	

PROBLEM 14-1 ___, Concluded

ACCOUNTS	BALANCE, ________, 2005	TRANSACTIONS		BALANCE, ________, 2006
		DEBIT	CREDIT	

PROBLEM 14-2 ___

Omit "00" in the cents columns.

PROBLEM 14-2 ___, Continued

PROBLEM 14-2 ___, Continued

The use of this form is not required unless so indicated by the instructor.

Work Sheet for Statement of Cash Flows

ACCOUNTS	BALANCE, DEC. 31, 2005	TRANSACTIONS		BALANCE, DEC. 31, 2006
		DEBIT	CREDIT	

PROBLEM 14-2 ___, Concluded

ACCOUNTS	BALANCE, DEC. 31, 2005	TRANSACTIONS DEBIT	TRANSACTIONS CREDIT	BALANCE, DEC. 31, 2006

PROBLEM 14-3 ___

Omit "00" in the cents columns.

PROBLEM 14-3 ___, Continued

Name ______________________________

PROBLEM 14-3 ___, Continued

The use of this form is not required unless so indicated by the instructor.

Work Sheet for Statement of Cash Flows

ACCOUNTS	BALANCE, DEC. 31, 2005	TRANSACTIONS		BALANCE, DEC. 31, 2006
		DEBIT	CREDIT	

PROBLEM 14-3 ___, Concluded

ACCOUNTS	BALANCE, DEC. 31, 2005	TRANSACTIONS		BALANCE, DEC. 31, 2006
		DEBIT	CREDIT	

Name ______________________________

PROBLEM 14-4 ___

Omit "00" in the cents columns.

PROBLEM 14-4 ___, Continued

PROBLEM 14-4 ___, Continued

The use of this form is not required unless so indicated by the instructor.

Work Sheet for Statement of Cash Flows

ACCOUNTS	BALANCE, DEC. 31, 2006	TRANSACTIONS		BALANCE, DEC. 31, 2007
		DEBIT	CREDIT	

PROBLEM 14-4 ___, Concluded

ACCOUNTS	BALANCE, DEC. 31, 2006	TRANSACTIONS		BALANCE, DEC. 31, 2007
		DEBIT	CREDIT	

Name ____

PROBLEM 14-5 ___

Omit "00" in the cents columns.

PROBLEM 14-5 ___, Continued

PROBLEM 14-5 ___, Continued

The use of this form is not required unless so indicated by the instructor.

Work Sheet for Statement of Cash Flows

ACCOUNTS	BALANCE, ________, 2005	TRANSACTIONS DEBIT	TRANSACTIONS CREDIT	BALANCE, ________, 2006

PROBLEM 14-5 ___, Concluded

ACCOUNTS	BALANCE, ________, 2005	TRANSACTIONS DEBIT	TRANSACTIONS CREDIT	BALANCE, ________, 2006

EXERCISE 15-1

a.

	2006		2005	
	AMOUNT	PERCENT	AMOUNT	PERCENT

b.

EXERCISE 15-2

a.

	FISCAL YEAR 2002		FISCAL YEAR 2001	
	AMOUNT	PERCENT	AMOUNT	PERCENT

b.

EXERCISE 15-3

a.

	HORIZON PUBLISHING COMPANY		PUBLISHING INDUSTRY AVERAGE
	AMOUNT	PERCENT	PERCENT

b.

EXERCISE 15-4

	2006		2005	
	AMOUNT	PERCENT	AMOUNT	PERCENT

EXERCISE 15-5

a.

	2006	2005	INCREASE (DECREASE)	
	AMOUNT	AMOUNT	AMOUNT	PERCENT

b.

EXERCISE 15-6

a. (1)

(2)

(3)

b.

EXERCISE 15-7

a. (1)

(2)

b.

EXERCISE 15-8

a. ______________________________

b. ______________________________

EXERCISE 15-9

a. (1)

(2)

b.

EXERCISE 15-10

a. (1)

(2)

b.

EXERCISE 15-11

a. (1)

(2)

b.

EXERCISE 15-12

a. (1) ______________________________

(2) ______________________________

b. ______________________________

EXERCISE 15-13

a.

b.

c.

EXERCISE 15-14

a. ______________________

b. ______________________

c. ______________________

EXERCISE 15-15

a.

b.

c.

EXERCISE 15-16

a. ______________________________

b._

EXERCISE 15-17

a.

b.

Name ______________________________

EXERCISE 15-18

a. ______________________________

b. ______________________________

c. ______________________________

d. ______________________________

EXERCISE 15-19

a.

b.

c.

d.

e.

f.

Name ______________________________

EXERCISE 15-20

a.

b.

c.

d.

e.

f.

EXERCISE 15-21

a.

b.

c.

d.

EXERCISE 15-22

a.

b.

EXERCISE 15-23

a.

b.

Name ____________________

PROBLEM 15-1 ___

1.

Comparative Income Statement

	2006	2005	INCREASE (DECREASE)	
			AMOUNT	PERCENT

PROBLEM 15-1 ___, Concluded

2.

PROBLEM 15-2 ___

1.

Comparative Income Statement

	2006		2005	
	AMOUNT	PERCENT	AMOUNT	PERCENT

PROBLEM 15-2 ___, Concluded

2.

PROBLEM 15-3 ___

1. a. ______________________________

b. ______________________________

c. ______________________________

PROBLEM 15-3 ___, Concluded

2.

Transaction	Working Capital	Current Ratio	Quick Ratio
a.			
b.			
c.			
d.			
e.			
f.			
g.			
h.			
i.			
j.			

Supporting calculations:

Name ______________________________________

PROBLEM 15-4 ___

1. through 19.

PROBLEM 15-4 ___, Concluded

PROBLEM 15-5 ___

1. a.

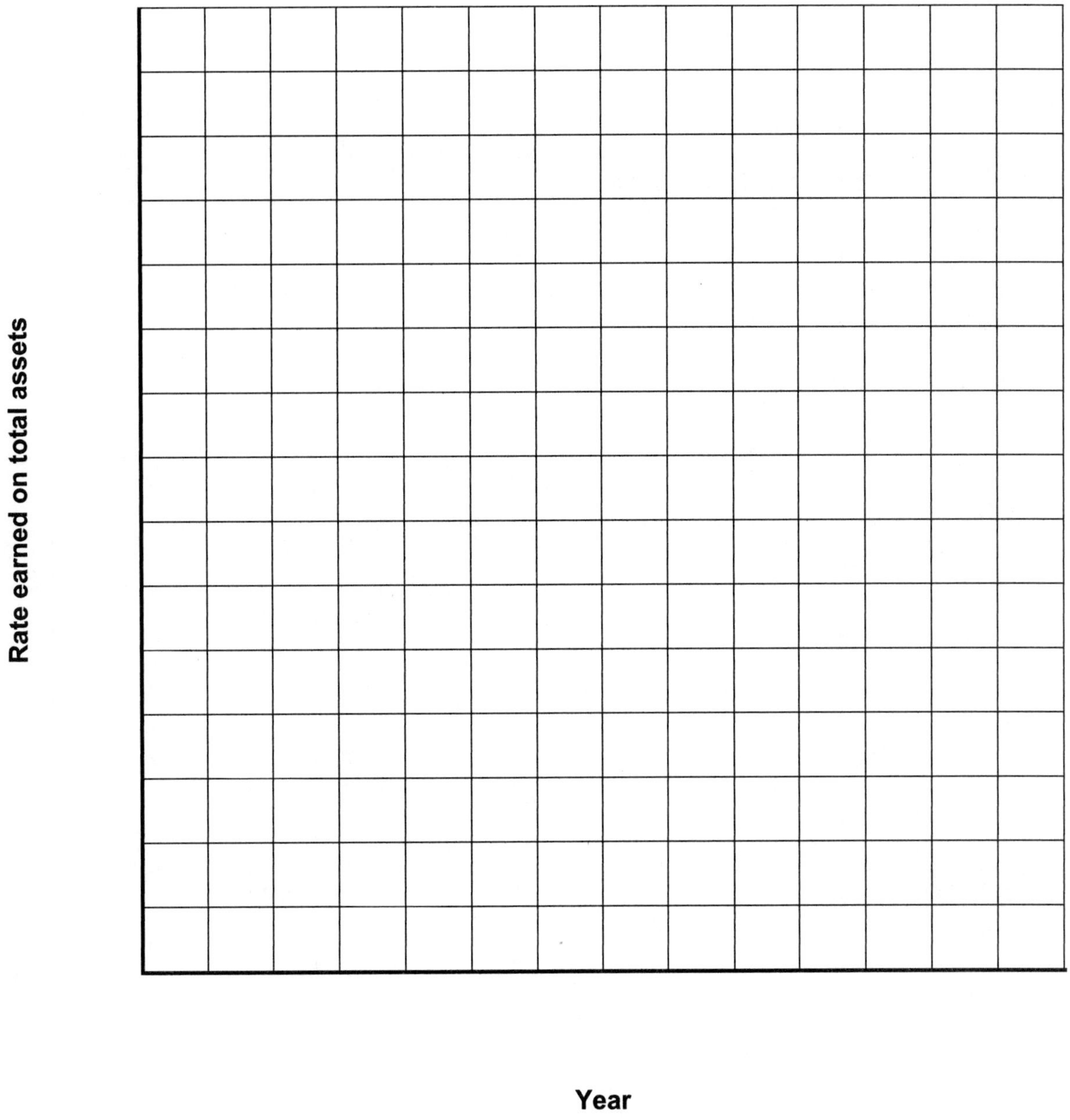

PROBLEM 15-5 ___, Continued

1. b.

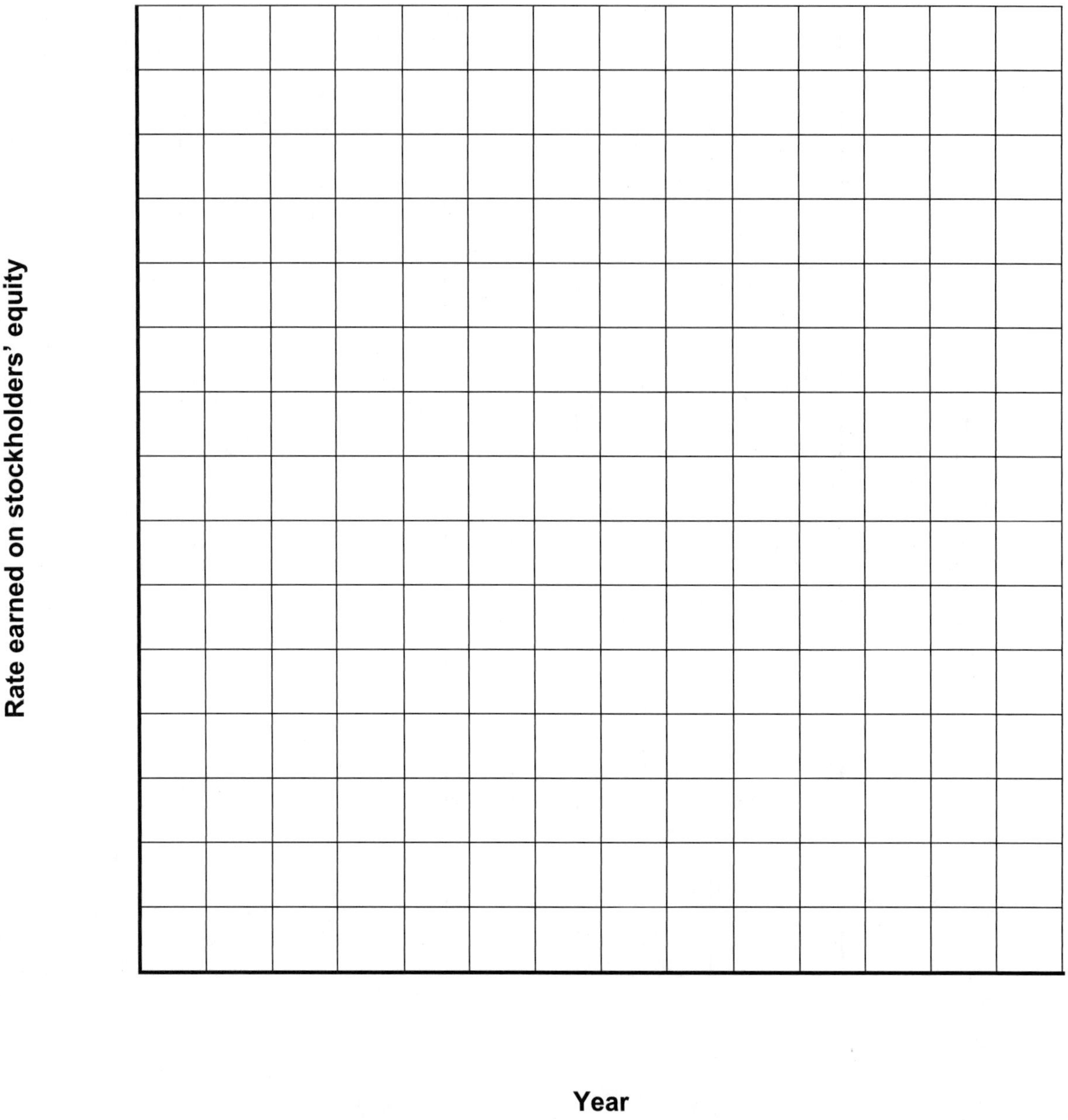

PROBLEM 15-5 ___, Continued

1. c.

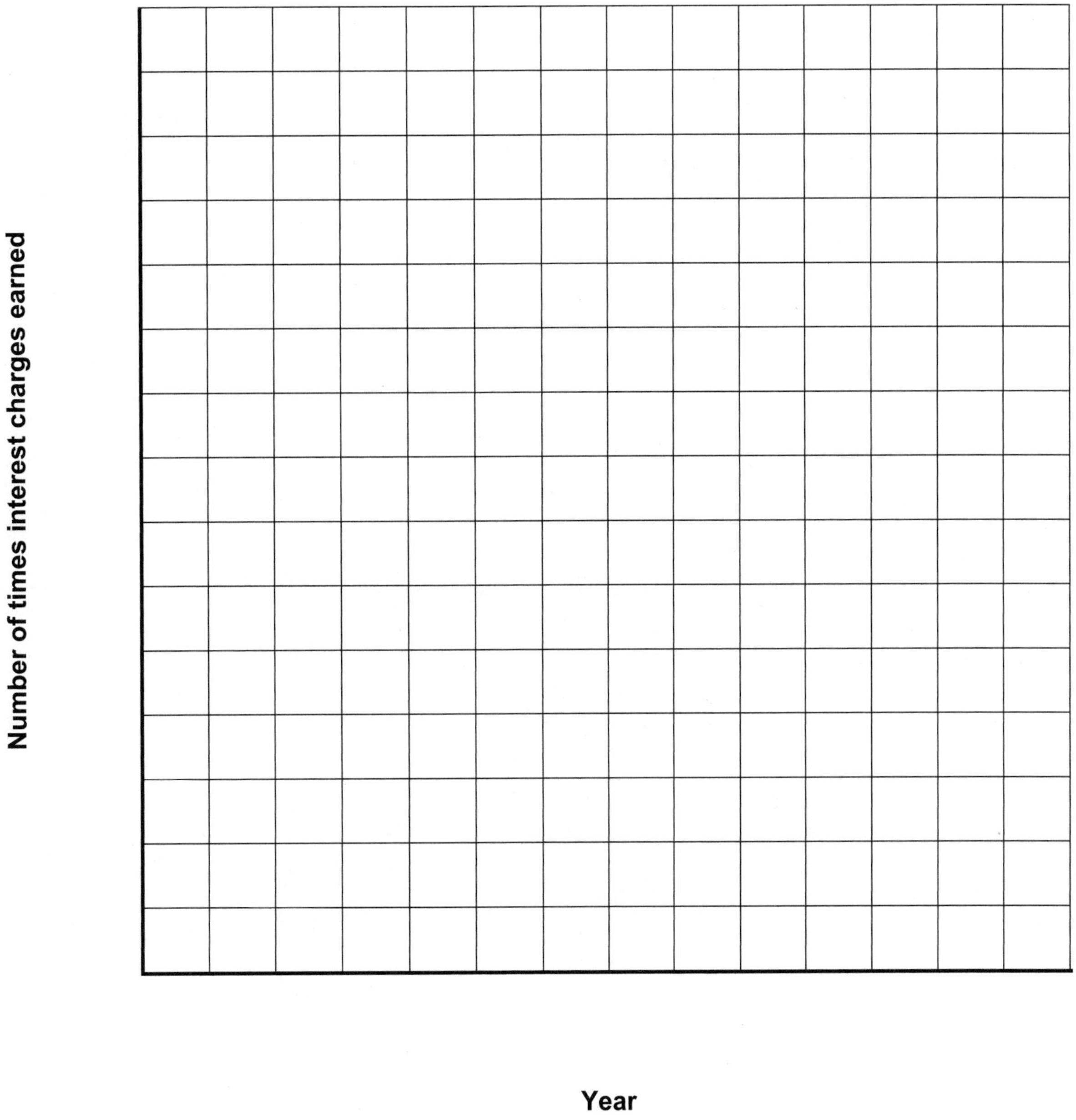

PROBLEM 15-5 ___, Continued

1. d.

Ratio of liabilities to stockholders' equity

Year

PROBLEM 15-5 ___, Continued

2.

PROBLEM 15-5 ___, Concluded

HOME DEPOT, INC., PROBLEM

1. a. through m.

HOME DEPOT, INC., PROBLEM, Continued

HOME DEPOT, INC., PROBLEM, Continued

2. a. through m.

HOME DEPOT, INC., PROBLEM, Concluded

EXERCISE B-1

a.

Office Supplies		*Office Supplies Expense*	

b.

Office Supplies		*Office Supplies Expense*	

EXERCISE B-2

a. and b.

JOURNAL PAGE

	DATE		DESCRIPTION	POST. REF.	DEBIT	CREDIT	
1							1
2							2
3							3
4							4
5							5
6							6
7							7
8							8
9							9
10							10
11							11
12							12
13							13
14							14
15							15
16							16
17							17
18							18
19							19
20							20
21							21

EXERCISE B-3

a.

Unearned Advertising Revenue

Advertising Revenue

b.

Unearned Advertising Revenue

Advertising Revenue

EXERCISE B-4

JOURNAL

PAGE

	DATE		DESCRIPTION	POST. REF.	DEBIT	CREDIT	
1							1
2							2
3							3
4							4
5							5
6							6
7							7
8							8
9							9
10							10
11							11
12							12
13							13
14							14
15							15
16							16
17							17
18							18
19							19
20							20
21							21
22							22

PROBLEM C-1

1. ________________________

2. **PURCHASES JOURNAL**

PROBLEM C-1, Concluded

REVENUE JOURNAL

3.

Name ______________________________

PROBLEM C-2

a. Adjustment to record accrued salaries at the end of the year: ______________________________

____

b. Receipt of cash on account from a customer: ______________________________

____

c. Providing services on account: ______________________________

____

d. Issuance of additional capital stock in exchange for cash: ______________________________

____

e. Receipt of cash for rent: ______________________________

____

f. Receipt of cash refund from overpayment of taxes: ______________________________

____

g. Closing of dividends account at the end of the year: ______________________________

____

h. Sale of office supplies on account, at cost, to a neighboring business: ______________________________

____

i. Receipt of cash from sale of office equipment: ______________________________

____

j. Providing services for cash: ______________________________

____

Page not used.

Name ______________________________

PROBLEM C-3

a. ______________________________

b. ______________________________

c. ______________________________

d. ______________________________

e. ______________________________

f. ______________________________

g. ______________________________

h. ______________________________

i. ______________________________

j. ______________________________

k. ______________________________

l. ______________________________

m. ______________________________

Page not used.

Name ________________________________

PROBLEM C-4

1. and 2.

REVENUE JOURNAL

PAGE *1*

DATE		INVOICE NO.	ACCOUNT DEBITED	POST. REF.	ACCTS. REC. DR. FEES EARNED CR.

PROBLEM C-4, Continued

JOURNAL

PAGE *1*

DATE		DESCRIPTION	POST. REF.	DEBIT	CREDIT

Name ____________________________________

PROBLEM C-4, Continued

ACCOUNTS RECEIVABLE LEDGER

NAME

ADDRESS

DATE		ITEM	POST. REF.	DEBIT	CREDIT	BALANCE

NAME

ADDRESS

DATE		ITEM	POST. REF.	DEBIT	CREDIT	BALANCE

NAME

ADDRESS

DATE		ITEM	POST. REF.	DEBIT	CREDIT	BALANCE

NAME

ADDRESS

DATE		ITEM	POST. REF.	DEBIT	CREDIT	BALANCE

NAME

ADDRESS

DATE		ITEM	POST. REF.	DEBIT	CREDIT	BALANCE

PROBLEM C-4, Concluded

2.

GENERAL LEDGER

ACCOUNT *Accounts Receivable* ACCOUNT NO. *12*

DATE		ITEM	POST. REF.	DEBIT	CREDIT	BALANCE	
						DEBIT	CREDIT

ACCOUNT *Supplies* ACCOUNT NO. *13*

DATE		ITEM	POST. REF.	DEBIT	CREDIT	BALANCE	
						DEBIT	CREDIT

ACCOUNT *Fees Earned* ACCOUNT NO. *41*

DATE		ITEM	POST. REF.	DEBIT	CREDIT	BALANCE	
						DEBIT	CREDIT

3. a. $ ____________________

b. $ ____________________

4.

____

____

____

____

____

____

Name ______________________________________

PROBLEM C-5

1. and 5.

GENERAL LEDGER

ACCOUNT *Cash* ACCOUNT NO. *11*

DATE	ITEM	POST. REF.	DEBIT	CREDIT	BALANCE	
					DEBIT	CREDIT

ACCOUNT *Accounts Receivable* ACCOUNT NO. *12*

DATE	ITEM	POST. REF.	DEBIT	CREDIT	BALANCE	
					DEBIT	CREDIT

ACCOUNT *Notes Receivable* ACCOUNT NO. *14*

DATE	ITEM	POST. REF.	DEBIT	CREDIT	BALANCE	
					DEBIT	CREDIT

ACCOUNT *Fees Earned* ACCOUNT NO. *41*

DATE	ITEM	POST. REF.	DEBIT	CREDIT	BALANCE	
					DEBIT	CREDIT

PROBLEM C-5, Continued

2. and 4.

ACCOUNTS RECEIVABLE SUBSIDIARY LEDGER

NAME

ADDRESS

DATE		ITEM	POST. REF.	DEBIT	CREDIT	BALANCE

NAME

ADDRESS

DATE		ITEM	POST. REF.	DEBIT	CREDIT	BALANCE

NAME

ADDRESS

DATE		ITEM	POST. REF.	DEBIT	CREDIT	BALANCE

NAME

ADDRESS

DATE		ITEM	POST. REF.	DEBIT	CREDIT	BALANCE

Name ______________________________

PROBLEM C-5, Continued

3., 4., and 5.

REVENUE JOURNAL

PAGE *40*

DATE		INVOICE NO.	ACCOUNT DEBITED	POST. REF.	ACCTS. REC. DR. FEES EARNED CR.

CASH RECEIPTS JOURNAL

PAGE *36*

DATE		ACCOUNT CREDITED	POST. REF.	FEES EARNED CR.	ACCOUNTS REC. CR.	CASH DR.

PROBLEM C-5, Concluded

JOURNAL

PAGE *1*

	DATE		DESCRIPTION	POST. REF.	DEBIT	CREDIT	
1							1
2							2
3							3
4							4
5							5
6							6
7							7
8							8
9							9
10							10
11							11
12							12
13							13
14							14
15							15
16							16
17							17
18							18
19							19
20							20
21							21
22							22
23							23
24							24
25							25
26							26
27							27
28							28
29							29
30							30

6.

Name ______________________________

PROBLEM C-6

1. and 4.

GENERAL LEDGER

ACCOUNT *Field Supplies* ACCOUNT NO. *14*

DATE	ITEM	POST. REF.	DEBIT	CREDIT	BALANCE DEBIT	BALANCE CREDIT

ACCOUNT *Office Supplies* ACCOUNT NO. *15*

DATE	ITEM	POST. REF.	DEBIT	CREDIT	BALANCE DEBIT	BALANCE CREDIT

ACCOUNT *Office Equipment* ACCOUNT NO. *18*

DATE	ITEM	POST. REF.	DEBIT	CREDIT	BALANCE DEBIT	BALANCE CREDIT

ACCOUNT *Accounts Payable* ACCOUNT NO. *21*

DATE	ITEM	POST. REF.	DEBIT	CREDIT	BALANCE DEBIT	BALANCE CREDIT

PROBLEM C-6, Continued

2. and 3.

ACCOUNTS PAYABLE SUBSIDIARY LEDGER

NAME

ADDRESS

DATE		ITEM	POST. REF.	DEBIT	CREDIT	BALANCE

NAME

ADDRESS

DATE		ITEM	POST. REF.	DEBIT	CREDIT	BALANCE

NAME

ADDRESS

DATE		ITEM	POST. REF.	DEBIT	CREDIT	BALANCE

Name ______________________________

PROBLEM C-6, Continued

NAME

ADDRESS

DATE		ITEM	POST. REF.	DEBIT	CREDIT	BALANCE

NAME

ADDRESS

DATE		ITEM	POST. REF.	DEBIT	CREDIT	BALANCE

PROBLEM C-6, Concluded

3. and 4.

PURCHASES JOURNAL

PAGE *30*

	DATE		ACCOUNT CREDITED	POST. REF.	ACCOUNTS PAYABLE CR.	FIELD SUPPLIES DR.	OFFICE SUPPLIES DR.	OTHER ACCOUNTS DR.			
								ACCOUNT	POST. REF.	AMOUNT	
1											1
2											2
3											3
4											4
5											5
6											6
7											7
8											8
9											9
10											10
11											11
12											12
13											13
14											14
15											15
16											16
17											17
18											18
19											19
20											20

5. a. $ ______________________

b. $ ______________________

PROBLEM C-7

1., 2., and 3.

PURCHASES JOURNAL

PAGE *1*

	DATE	ACCOUNT CREDITED	POST. REF.	ACCOUNTS PAYABLE CR.	FIELD SUPPLIES DR.	OFFICE SUPPLIES DR.	OTHER ACCOUNTS DR. ACCOUNT	OTHER ACCOUNTS DR. POST. REF.	OTHER ACCOUNTS DR. AMOUNT	
1										1
2										2
3										3
4										4
5										5
6										6
7										7
8										8
9										9
10										10
11										11
12										12
13										13
14										14
15										15
16										16
17										17
18										18
19										19
20										20
21										21
22										22
23										23

PROBLEM C-7, Continued

CASH PAYMENTS JOURNAL

PAGE *1*

	DATE	CK. NO.	ACCOUNT DEBITED	POST. REF.	OTHER ACCOUNTS DR.	ACCOUNTS PAYABLE DR.	CASH CR.	
1								1
2								2
3								3
4								4
5								5
6								6
7								7
8								8
9								9
10								10
11								11
12								12
13								13
14								14
15								15
16								16
17								17

1. and 2.

JOURNAL

PAGE *1*

	DATE	DESCRIPTION	POST. REF.	DEBIT	CREDIT	
1						1
2						2
3						3
4						4
5						5
6						6
7						7
8						8
9						9
10						10
11						11
12						12
13						13

PROBLEM C-7, Continued

1.

ACCOUNTS PAYABLE SUBSIDIARY LEDGER

NAME

ADDRESS

DATE		ITEM	POST. REF.	DEBIT	CREDIT	BALANCE

NAME

ADDRESS

DATE		ITEM	POST. REF.	DEBIT	CREDIT	BALANCE

NAME

ADDRESS

DATE		ITEM	POST. REF.	DEBIT	CREDIT	BALANCE

PROBLEM C-7, Continued

2. and 3.

GENERAL LEDGER

ACCOUNT *Cash* ACCOUNT NO. *11*

DATE		ITEM	POST. REF.	DEBIT	CREDIT	BALANCE	
						DEBIT	CREDIT

ACCOUNT *Field Supplies* ACCOUNT NO. *14*

DATE		ITEM	POST. REF.	DEBIT	CREDIT	BALANCE	
						DEBIT	CREDIT

ACCOUNT *Office Supplies* ACCOUNT NO. *15*

DATE		ITEM	POST. REF.	DEBIT	CREDIT	BALANCE	
						DEBIT	CREDIT

ACCOUNT *Field Equipment* ACCOUNT NO. *17*

DATE		ITEM	POST. REF.	DEBIT	CREDIT	BALANCE	
						DEBIT	CREDIT

PROBLEM C-7, Continued

ACCOUNT *Land* ACCOUNT NO. *19*

DATE	ITEM	POST. REF.	DEBIT	CREDIT	BALANCE	
					DEBIT	CREDIT

ACCOUNT *Accounts Payable* ACCOUNT NO. *21*

DATE	ITEM	POST. REF.	DEBIT	CREDIT	BALANCE	
					DEBIT	CREDIT

ACCOUNT *Salary Expense* ACCOUNT NO. *61*

DATE	ITEM	POST. REF.	DEBIT	CREDIT	BALANCE	
					DEBIT	CREDIT

ACCOUNT *Rent Expense* ACCOUNT NO. *71*

DATE	ITEM	POST. REF.	DEBIT	CREDIT	BALANCE	
					DEBIT	CREDIT

PROBLEM C-7, Concluded

4.

Name ____________________

PROBLEM C-8

1., 3., and 4.

GENERAL LEDGER

ACCOUNT *Cash* ACCOUNT NO. *11*

DATE	ITEM	POST. REF.	DEBIT	CREDIT	BALANCE DEBIT	BALANCE CREDIT

ACCOUNT *Accounts Receivable* ACCOUNT NO. *12*

DATE	ITEM	POST. REF.	DEBIT	CREDIT	BALANCE DEBIT	BALANCE CREDIT

ACCOUNT *Maintenance Supplies* ACCOUNT NO. *14*

DATE	ITEM	POST. REF.	DEBIT	CREDIT	BALANCE DEBIT	BALANCE CREDIT

ACCOUNT *Office Supplies* ACCOUNT NO. *15*

DATE	ITEM	POST. REF.	DEBIT	CREDIT	BALANCE DEBIT	BALANCE CREDIT

PROBLEM C-8, Continued

ACCOUNT *Office Equipment* ACCOUNT NO. *16*

DATE		ITEM	POST. REF.	DEBIT	CREDIT	BALANCE	
						DEBIT	CREDIT

ACCOUNT *Accumulated Depreciation—Office Equipment* ACCOUNT NO. *17*

DATE		ITEM	POST. REF.	DEBIT	CREDIT	BALANCE	
						DEBIT	CREDIT

ACCOUNT *Vehicles* ACCOUNT NO. *18*

DATE		ITEM	POST. REF.	DEBIT	CREDIT	BALANCE	
						DEBIT	CREDIT

ACCOUNT *Accumulated Depreciation—Vehicles* ACCOUNT NO. *19*

DATE		ITEM	POST. REF.	DEBIT	CREDIT	BALANCE	
						DEBIT	CREDIT

PROBLEM C-8, Continued

ACCOUNT *Accounts Payable* ACCOUNT NO. *21*

DATE		ITEM	POST. REF.	DEBIT	CREDIT	BALANCE	
						DEBIT	CREDIT

ACCOUNT *Capital Stock* ACCOUNT NO. *31*

DATE		ITEM	POST. REF.	DEBIT	CREDIT	BALANCE	
						DEBIT	CREDIT

ACCOUNT *Retained Earnings* ACCOUNT NO. *32*

DATE		ITEM	POST. REF.	DEBIT	CREDIT	BALANCE	
						DEBIT	CREDIT

ACCOUNT *Fees Earned* ACCOUNT NO. *41*

DATE		ITEM	POST. REF.	DEBIT	CREDIT	BALANCE	
						DEBIT	CREDIT

PROBLEM C-8, Continued

ACCOUNT *Driver Salaries Expense* ACCOUNT NO. *51*

DATE	ITEM	POST. REF.	DEBIT	CREDIT	BALANCE DEBIT	BALANCE CREDIT

ACCOUNT *Maintenance Supplies Expense* ACCOUNT NO. *52*

DATE	ITEM	POST. REF.	DEBIT	CREDIT	BALANCE DEBIT	BALANCE CREDIT

ACCOUNT *Fuel Expense* ACCOUNT NO. *53*

DATE	ITEM	POST. REF.	DEBIT	CREDIT	BALANCE DEBIT	BALANCE CREDIT

ACCOUNT *Office Salaries Expense* ACCOUNT NO. *61*

DATE	ITEM	POST. REF.	DEBIT	CREDIT	BALANCE DEBIT	BALANCE CREDIT

PROBLEM C-8, Continued

ACCOUNT *Rent Expense* ACCOUNT NO. *62*

DATE		ITEM	POST. REF.	DEBIT	CREDIT	BALANCE DEBIT	BALANCE CREDIT

ACCOUNT *Advertising Expense* ACCOUNT NO. *63*

DATE		ITEM	POST. REF.	DEBIT	CREDIT	BALANCE DEBIT	BALANCE CREDIT

ACCOUNT *Miscellaneous Administrative Expense* ACCOUNT NO. *64*

DATE		ITEM	POST. REF.	DEBIT	CREDIT	BALANCE DEBIT	BALANCE CREDIT

PROBLEM C-8, Continued

2., 3., and 4.

PURCHASES JOURNAL

PAGE 37

	DATE	ACCOUNT CREDITED	POST. REF.	ACCOUNTS PAYABLE CR.	MAINTENANCE SUPPLIES DR.	OFFICE SUPPLIES DR.	OTHER ACCOUNTS DR. ACCOUNT	OTHER ACCOUNTS DR. POST. REF.	OTHER ACCOUNTS DR. AMOUNT	
1										1
2										2
3										3
4										4
5										5
6										6
7										7
8										8
9										9
10										10
11										11
12										12
13										13
14										14
15										15
16										16
17										17
18										18
19										19
20										20
21										21
22										22
23										23

PROBLEM C-8, Continued

CASH RECEIPTS JOURNAL

PAGE *31*

	DATE		ACCOUNT CREDITED	POST. REF.	OTHER ACCOUNTS CR.	ACCOUNTS REC. CR.	CASH DR.	
1								1
2								2
3								3
4								4
5								5
6								6
7								7
8								8
9								9
10								10
11								11
12								12
13								13
14								14
15								15
16								16

2. and 4.

REVENUE JOURNAL

PAGE *35*

	DATE		INVOICE NO.	ACCOUNT DEBITED	POST. REF.	ACCTS. REC. DR. FEES EARNED CR.	
1							1
2							2
3							3
4							4
5							5
6							6
7							7
8							8
9							9
10							10
11							11
12							12
13							13
14							14

PROBLEM C-8, Continued

2., 3., and 4.

CASH PAYMENTS JOURNAL

PAGE *34*

	DATE	CK. NO.	ACCOUNT DEBITED	POST. REF.	OTHER ACCOUNTS DR.	ACCOUNTS PAYABLE DR.	CASH CR.	
1								1
2								2
3								3
4								4
5								5
6								6
7								7
8								8
9								9
10								10
11								11
12								12
13								13
14								14
15								15
16								16
17								17
18								18
19								19

2. and 3.

JOURNAL

PAGE *1*

	DATE	DESCRIPTION	POST. REF.	DEBIT	CREDIT	
1						1
2						2
3						3
4						4
5						5
6						6
7						7
8						8
9						9
10						10
11						11

PROBLEM C-8, Concluded

5.

6. Balance of accounts receivable controlling account: $ ________

Balance of accounts payable controlling account: $ ________

Page not used.

EXERCISE D-1

a.–e.

JOURNAL

PAGE

	DATE	DESCRIPTION	POST. REF.	DEBIT	CREDIT	
1						1
2						2
3						3
4						4
5						5
6						6
7						7
8						8
9						9
10						10
11						11
12						12
13						13
14						14
15						15
16						16
17						17

EXERCISE D-2

JOURNAL

PAGE

	DATE	DESCRIPTION	POST. REF.	DEBIT	CREDIT	
1						1
2						2
3						3
4						4
5						5
6						6
7						7
8						8
9						9
10						10
11						11
12						12
13						13

EXERCISE D-3

JOURNAL

PAGE

	DATE		DESCRIPTION	POST. REF.	DEBIT	CREDIT	
1							1
2							2
3							3
4							4
5							5
6							6
7							7
8							8
9							9
10							10
11							11
12							12
13							13
14							14
15							15

EXERCISE D-4

a. Sales – (X + Y) = Net sales

b.Purchases – (X + Y) = Net purchases

c. Net purchases + X = Cost of merchandise purchased

d. Merchandise inventory (beginning) + Cost of merchandise purchased = X

e. Merchandise available for sale – X = Cost of merchandise sold

f. Net sales – Cost of merchandise sold = X

g. Gross profit – Operating expenses = X

h. X + Y = Operating expenses

i. Income from operations + X – Y = Net income

Name ______________________________

EXERCISE D-5

EXERCISE D-6

a. and b.

JOURNAL

PAGE

DATE		DESCRIPTION	POST. REF.	DEBIT	CREDIT

Name ______________________________

PROBLEM D-1

JOURNAL

PAGE

DATE	DESCRIPTION	POST. REF.	DEBIT	CREDIT

PROBLEM D-1, Concluded

JOURNAL

PAGE

DATE	DESCRIPTION	POST. REF.	DEBIT	CREDIT

Name ______________________

PROBLEM D-2

JOURNAL

PAGE

DATE		DESCRIPTION	POST. REF.	DEBIT	CREDIT

PROBLEM D-2, Concluded

JOURNAL

PAGE

DATE		DESCRIPTION	POST. REF.	DEBIT	CREDIT

Name ______________________________

PROBLEM D-3

1.

JOURNAL

PAGE

DATE	DESCRIPTION	POST. REF.	DEBIT	CREDIT

PROBLEM D-3, Concluded

2.

JOURNAL

PAGE

DATE		DESCRIPTION	POST. REF.	DEBIT	CREDIT

Name ______________________________________

PROBLEM D-4

1. *Use the 10-column work sheets found on pages 590–591 and 594–595.*

PROBLEM D-4, Continued

	ACCOUNT TITLE	TRIAL BALANCE		ADJUSTMENTS		
		DEBIT	CREDIT	DEBIT	CREDIT	
1						1
2						2
3						3
4						4
5						5
6						6
7						7
8						8
9						9
10						10
11						11
12						12
13						13
14						14
15						15
16						16
17						17
18						18
19						19
20						20
21						21
22						22
23						23
24						24
25						25
26						26
27						27
28						28
29						29
30						30
31						31
32						32
33						33
34						34
35						35
36						36
37						37

Name ______________________________________

PROBLEM D-4, Continued

____

____

____

	ADJUSTED TRIAL BALANCE		INCOME STATEMENT		BALANCE SHEET		
	DEBIT	CREDIT	DEBIT	CREDIT	DEBIT	CREDIT	
1							1
2							2
3							3
4							4
5							5
6							6
7							7
8							8
9							9
10							10
11							11
12							12
13							13
14							14
15							15
16							16
17							17
18							18
19							19
20							20
21							21
22							22
23							23
24							24
25							25
26							26
27							27
28							28
29							29
30							30
31							31
32							32
33							33
34							34
35							35
36							36
37							37

Page not used.

Page not used.

PROBLEM D-4, Continued

ACCOUNT TITLE	TRIAL BALANCE		ADJUSTMENTS	
	DEBIT	CREDIT	DEBIT	CREDIT

Name ______________________________

PROBLEM D-4, Continued

____

____

	ADJUSTED TRIAL BALANCE		INCOME STATEMENT		BALANCE SHEET		
	DEBIT	CREDIT	DEBIT	CREDIT	DEBIT	CREDIT	
1							1
2							2
3							3
4							4
5							5
6							6
7							7
8							8
9							9
10							10
11							11
12							12
13							13
14							14
15							15
16							16
17							17
18							18
19							19
20							20
21							21
22							22
23							23
24							24
25							25
26							26
27							27
28							28
29							29
30							30
31							31
32							32
33							33
34							34
35							35
36							36
37							37

Page not used.

Name ______________________________

PROBLEM D-4, Continued

2. *Omit "00" in the cents columns.*

PROBLEM D-4, Continued

Name ______________________________

PROBLEM D-4, Continued

3. *Omit "00" in the cents columns.*

PROBLEM D-4, Continued

4. *Omit "00" in the cents columns.*

PROBLEM D-4, Continued

5.

JOURNAL

PAGE

	DATE		DESCRIPTION	POST. REF.	DEBIT	CREDIT	
1							1
2							2
3							3
4							4
5							5
6							6
7							7
8							8
9							9
10							10
11							11
12							12
13							13
14							14
15							15
16							16
17							17
18							18
19							19
20							20
21							21
22							22
23							23
24							24
25							25
26							26
27							27
28							28
29							29
30							30
31							31
32							32
33							33
34							34
35							35
36							36

PROBLEM D-4, Concluded

6.

JOURNAL

PAGE

	DATE	DESCRIPTION	POST. REF.	DEBIT	CREDIT	
1						1
2						2
3						3
4						4
5						5
6						6
7						7
8						8
9						9
10						10
11						11
12						12
13						13
14						14
15						15
16						16
17						17
18						18
19						19
20						20
21						21
22						22
23						23
24						24
25						25
26						26
27						27
28						28
29						29
30						30
31						31
32						32
33						33
34						34
35						35
36						36

Name ______________________________

EXERCISE E-1

JOURNAL

PAGE

DATE		DESCRIPTION	POST. REF.	DEBIT	CREDIT

EXERCISE E-2

JOURNAL PAGE

DATE		DESCRIPTION	POST. REF.	DEBIT	CREDIT

Name ______________________________

PROBLEM E-1

1. and 2.

JOURNAL

PAGE

DATE	DESCRIPTION	POST. REF.	DEBIT	CREDIT

PROBLEM E-1, Concluded

JOURNAL

PAGE

	DATE		DESCRIPTION	POST. REF.	DEBIT	CREDIT	
1							1
2							2
3							3
4							4
5							5
6							6
7							7
8							8
9							9
10							10
11							11
12							12
13							13
14							14
15							15
16							16
17							17
18							18
19							19
20							20
21							21
22							22
23							23
24							24
25							25
26							26
27							27
28							28
29							29
30							30
31							31
32							32
33							33
34							34
35							35
36							36

JOURNAL PAGE

	DATE		DESCRIPTION	POST. REF.	DEBIT	CREDIT	
1							1
2							2
3							3
4							4
5							5
6							6
7							7
8							8
9							9
10							10
11							11
12							12
13							13
14							14
15							15
16							16
17							17
18							18
19							19
20							20
21							21
22							22
23							23
24							24
25							25
26							26
27							27
28							28
29							29
30							30
31							31
32							32
33							33
34							34
35							35
36							36
37							37